Joe Stahlkuppe

Pomeranians

Everything About Purchase, Care, Nutrition, Behavior, and Training

D1402200

CONTENTS

UNDERSTANDING THE POMERANIAN

It is ironic that such an open and clearly people-oriented little dog should have a history so shrouded by the veil of time and a lack of actual information. But such is the case with the Pomeranian, which takes his name from vague references to the old German province of Pomerania. It was in this Baltic-bordering and obscure region that early specimens of little spitz dogs were purported to originate.

Origin and History

Once thought a part of the Pomeranian origin-mystery, artifacts recovered from excavations in Greece—and other exotic, nonEuropean locations—depicting Pomlike dogs have largely been discounted as having any direct bearing on the breed. The German and European spitz dogs have far too much genetic similarity to the Pomeranian to be only partial ancestors. Pomeranians may not have come exclusively from Pomerania, but northern Europe can claim this breed as its own.

The Pomeranian owes his genetic makeup to that diverse group of sledding, hunting, and herding dogs that sprang from northern Europe, commonly lumped together as the spitz. His relatives, the Samoyed, the Norwegian Elkhound, and a number of other northern breeds certainly have proven their worth

as workers, companions, and pets. Even the Pomeranian's "big brother"—the Keeshond—once bearing the none-too-flattering name of "the overweight Pomeranian" by early English dog breeders—fits neatly into the worker-companion-pet spitz category.

Stemming from trusted working stock, another Pomeranian irony is that the Pom, as we know him today, is largely a British re-creation complete with ties to the royal family. Queen Victoria, having been exposed to the charm of the larger spitz dogs by her German grandmother, Queen Charlotte, returned from Italy in 1888 with Marco, a smallish spitzlike dog that had become a favorite of hers. So captivated was Victoria that she began breeding and exhibiting specimens of what had come to be called Pomeranians. Her dogs were smaller than the sturdy, 30-pounders of

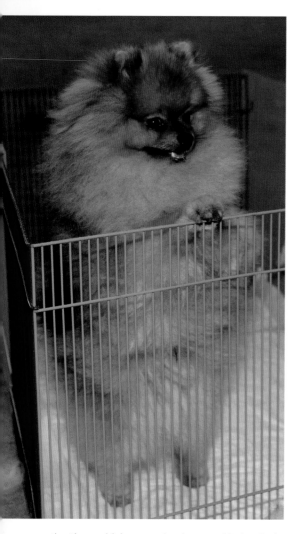

lighter Pomeranian, sometimes weighing only about one tenth as much.

The dog-loving public in England, and later in the United States, which had taken the name of a remote German province and shortened it into the fashionable Pom nickname, proceeded to do essentially the same thing with the breed itself. Without losing the jaunty spitz dog confidence and charisma, English dog breeders concentrated on the smallness craze and "breed 'em down in size" became the fancier's credo.

As with most fads, saner heads—and genetic practicality—finally prevailed and the Pomeranian size slide halted at about 5 pounds (2.3 kg) for a number of years. De-emphasizing diminutive size gave these early breeders the opportunity to develop other characteristics, such as improved coat quality, type, and symmetry. The German spitz dog thus became the raw ore from which the skillful British dog breeders shaped the Pomeranian. It was the English product that was exported to the United States in 1892 where the sprightly little breed soon developed, and has since maintained, a strong, dedicated following.

Pom Kin—Some Breeds Related to the Pomeranian
Keeshond
American Eskimo
The German Spitz Breeds
Schipperke
Samoyed
Akita
Norwegian Elkhound
Finnish Spitz

the time, which more closely resembled today's German spitz and American Eskimo dogs than the modern Poms. As a result of her interest in the breed, changes took place that would forever restructure the Pomeranian. The 30-pound (13.6 kg) spitz dog of Queen Victoria's grandmother began his transformation into the

British dog fanciers had created a beautiful miniature without sacrificing the attributes that had made the Pom's ancestors valuable workers in a much harsher environment. This exceptional product mixture of attractiveness, alertness, and adaptability combined in this "little big dog" to make the Pomeranian (male dogs we personalize for this book as *Hugo* and female Poms by the call-name *Prissy*) a winner—wherever he went.

Nature of the Pom

Whereas the Pomeranian may attract attention because of his appearance, he turns onlookers into admirers and many admirers into Pom owners because of his unique personality and an almost eerie ability to relate to his human beings. The latter quality is carried over from his ancestors' long association with humans and remains not only intact in the modern Pomeranian, but also close to the surface. The camaraderie with humans is one of the many reasons that *Pom people tend to remain Pom people.*

Pomeranians are very bright, both in intelligence and in personality. Poms can be stubborn and headstrong and need to understand that humans are in charge (see "Don't Let Your Pom Get the Upper Paw," page 80). As such, they need consistent human care and interaction to ensure that these quick-minded little dogs pick up the right habits and the correct behaviors. While usually not too difficult to housebreak, Poms do need careful and consistent housetraining to help them to reach their best level as good inside companion animals. Their keen alertness makes them reasonably easy to train. In fact, some Pomeranians

(see "Don't Let Your Pom Get the Upper Paw," page 80)

TIP

Service Activities Poms Can Do

Their small size notwithstanding, Pomeranians have functioned well in:

- Search and Rescue (especially in tight, confined spaces where larger dogs cannot go);
- Therapy Dog roles with hospitalized and elderly persons;
- Hearing assistance dogs.

---

do well in Obedience trials and other canine learning activities, where their saucy style and happy nature garner them many fans from among the onlookers.

Whether achieving in formal Obedience work or not, the well-trained and well-socialized Pomeranian is an excellent companion dog. His alertness and brave heart make the Pom

a fine early-warning watchdog quite capable of raising a bristling and outraged alarm at the first sign of an intruder. Appropriate training and encouragement are absolutely essential in teaching a young Pom the difference between a legitimate cause for a barking warning and the ordinary "things that go bump in the night" but that pose no danger to the dog or to its household.

Some dog breeders assert that the Pomeranian has canine insight into the moods and feelings of his owner. This apparent empathy causes Pom owners to cite instances in which their pets have picked up on subtle cues in a room or in a situation and acted in an appropriate matter. One owner, long accustomed to the same routine after work each night, found that his female Pomeranian also knew the schedule and would let out a bark if the owner strayed too far off the established time line. This behavior gives new meaning to the term "watchdog."

Characteristic Behavior

Pomeranians quickly put to rest any thought that they are merely animated stuffed animals totally dependent on their owners in every aspect of life. Pomeranians are pert, alert, independent (and acknowledged as sometimes stubborn) little dogs that possess clearly defined personalities that often seem to hark back to their northern dog ancestry. Poms behave much like their larger sled dog counterparts do, and often in an extremely independent fashion.

Pomeranians have a strong sense of personal property and enjoy their own special place or den within the home. This tendency can greatly ease crate-training and housetraining. Poms also take much pride in ownership of their belongings—toys, food and water dishes, and other items possessing a value known only to the dog. Although they are not usually quarrelsome in multidog households, Pomeranians do seem to want to make sure that their unique role in the home and their personal items are left undisturbed.

Kinship with Humans

The Pomeranian possesses a keenness of mind and a usual sweetness of spirit that has endeared the breed to millions of people the world over. His behavior seems consistent with his reputation as a superb companion dog. Hugo is seemingly endowed with a sense of propriety, and his behavior rarely is out of step with the situation. Poms are fun-loving dogs when fun is the order of the day and yet they can be more sedate when events demand calmer or quieter actions.

Owners of Pomeranians who have suffered a family death or some other loss have reported clearly sympathetic behavior from their dogs when sadness has been evident. Even Pom puppies seem to show this tendency. One owner reported an extremely reserved atmosphere surrounding a litter on the day one puppy had left for a new home.

Intelligence, Energy, and Loyalty

The Pomeranian is brave—sometimes too much so. As if unaware of his tininess, Hugo will bristle and sometimes even charge other, much larger dogs. Owners must make sure

CAUTION

Small Children and Poms

Small children, however well intended, can cause serious or even fatal injuries to tiny Pomeranians. Frightened little dogs can nip or bite children who hurt them in some way. Adults should always carefully supervise children with adult Poms and especially with fragile Pomeranian puppies.

that the little dog doesn't endanger himself by tackling a canine foe very much larger in size, if not in ferocity.

Hopefully, the Pom's actions are such that it stays just out of harm's way while actively making his displeasure abundantly and vocally clear. With humans, the Pomeranian is normally a friendly and happy dog that will make friends on his own terms and only after he is sure of one's intentions. Because of his intelligence and his high activity level, the Pomeranian needs to have his brightness and energy channeled into appropriate behaviors. With some simple, consistent training, the Pom can become an excellent watchdog, discerning unusual sounds from the ordinary.

No dog is more devoted to his owner than the Pomeranian. The breed's adaptability allows the Pomeranian to fit into life in an apartment, a suburban duplex, or even a rural home.

Although constraints *must* be placed on very young children—as should be the case with any of the toy breeds—the Pomeranian can become an excellent older child's pet as well as an incomparable companion for an older person. Given the almost uncanny ability of these little dogs to pick up on certain consistent cues and learn rather quickly what is expected of them, there are few breeds that can boast an overall better record of satisfied owners than the Pomeranian. As has been mentioned, this loyalty is amply demonstrated by the number of people who, after having owned a Pom, stay with the breed—enthusiastically.

Vocal Expression

Pomeranians are quite vocal little dogs. Their basic alertness makes them prone to barking. It is very important that all Poms be given adequate and consistent training to help them avoid becoming nuisance barkers. Whereas one Pomeranian may be a "yapper" and the next Pom may bark only when it is appropriate to do so, consistent training is *always* a valuable aid. A lack of careful and early training is generally the reason for most of the Poms that have been classified as noisy, as is probably the case with noisy dogs of any breed.

Adaptability

One of the strongest attributes of the Pomeranian is his ability to fit into his environment. To this end, he amply makes use of his mental and physical capacities. Breeders and owners like to point out how well many Poms do in Obedience work, in the show ring, as a companion dog, as a therapy dog, and as an alert home watchdog. Not surprisingly, these people are clearly convinced of superlatives about their Poms.

Most people who really get to know Poms have positive feelings about them. This speaks well for the image that the little dogs have established on trips outside their homes. Some of the staunchest supporters of the breed—other than their breeders and owners, of course—are those who have seen Poms in a different light from that of their owners. Even casual observers, who would be the most likely objective viewers of any breed, have a high positivity quotient about Pomeranians.

This adaptability of the Pomeranian was one of the reasons that British royalty was initially attracted to the little spitz dogs. That same adaptability remains one of the great strengths of the breed today and one of the key reasons

for the worldwide acceptance and popularity of the Pomeranian.

Mental Ability

Although the physical attractiveness of the Pomeranian, especially of puppies and show dogs, could account for a certain portion of the breed's great popularity, appearance is certainly not the sole reason. Cuteness and overall beauty will go only so far in assuring owner loyalty, either to an individual dog or to a specific breed.

The number of Poms in the Obedience ring, Rally, Agility, and other events speaks volumes about the way owners view the mental capacities of their little dogs. Success in these endeavors also strengthens the public perception of the Pom's intelligence and trainability. These trained-dog activities, done in strict accordance with appropriate rules and procedures, fall also under the close observation of a watchful audience. An opportunity to shine can quickly turn into a chance to do poorly—all right out there in public. That Poms and their owners are willing and able to sustain themselves and even thrive in such an environment gives good evidence of the smarts of the breed and the dedication of their trainers.

Less formal and less structured proof comes from Pomeranian owners and breeders. *Every* Pom owner seems to have an entire collection of stories illustrating great Pomeranian mental acuity. Another of the reasons cited by Queen Victoria for her attraction to and championing of the breed was its devotion and ample intelligence.

Pomeranians are very smart and as such bring a special responsibility to their owners or would-be owners. In order for Hugo to become the super pet, Obedience dog, show dog, or all-around companion that he can be, he will need early, firm, consistent treatment and adequate training.

Body Language

You have only to see a Pomeranian "strut his stuff" down an aisle at a dog show or "do his thing" in an Obedience or Agility event, to know that this tiny dog has a definite physical presence that almost magnetically draws the attention of onlookers. Pom owners claim that many Pomeranians rise to such occasions and actually show great enjoyment in being under the public scrutiny.

Pomeranians, although not normally hostile to other dogs, are not passive whiners either. When encountering a larger dog, the Pom may often bristle up his stiff and considerable coat, as if to make himself appear as large as possible. Hugo doesn't seem to know he isn't a Rottweiler and may actually be the aggressor. Help keep Hugo out of the trouble his pugilist self could get him into!

This behavior again seems to stem from actions commonly observed in other members of the extended spitz family of breeds. Initially, while in usually rough conditions, these Pomeranian ancestors were worker-sled dogs, and while pack behavior was always to be expected, indiscriminate battling was absolutely not to be tolerated. Dogs were valuable workers and fighting wasted both time and dogs.

Strangers

Human strangers often get much the same reception from the Pomeranian as strange

dogs do. The Pom will vocally make his presence known, often remaining a safe distance away, clearly analyzing the human being as to intent. Pomeranians often remember perceived friends and foes. This memory makes early and consistent socialization and training of puppies all the more essential. A lack of awareness by someone with such a perceptive little dog can lead to lingering misunderstandings. Whereas some breeds will accept almost any person as an immediate friend, the Pom is a bit more reticent and cautious. This is clearly illustrated in his body language.

When confronted with a new person, Hugo often will dance away from early attempts by a stranger to pet him or to pick him up. This is seen in even very young puppies who will stay coyly just out of reach until, almost as if by some secret signal, acceptance is magically bestowed upon the human. The boundaries and "no man's land" imposed by the Pom become decreasingly small until the friendly dog or puppy is within easy grasp. The Pomeranian loves attention and petting, but this "come hither, go yonder" routine makes it clear that any interaction will be strictly on Hugo's terms.

The Sensory Organs

As one might suspect with any breed as keen and bright as the Pomeranian, the breed possesses exceptional sensory abilities. The terms *alert* and *foxlike* have been used aptly to describe these diminutive canines. These terms scarcely could apply to a sluggish, inactive dog or to a member of a breed that fashion had left less than ready to face the world by adding flop ears or heavy bangs or other sensory-undermining or numbing characteristics. Sharp eyes, excellent hearing, and a surprising acuity in sense of smell have made the Pom the alert little dog that he is.

Eyes and Ears

The large, expressive eyes of the Pomeranian are among the first physical aspects that one notices about the breed. Large eyes enable Hugo to ably survey his domain and be instantly aware of things in his surroundings. Exceptional vision was key to the original spitzen roles of Hugo's far distant sled dog and herding dog ancestors. A heritage of keen eyesight is certainly one of the reasons for the Pomeranian's general success in the competitive dog/handler activities. This intelligent little dog doesn't miss much.

The ears of the Pomeranian also remain much like those of his sled dog ancestors, attractive yet utilitarian. They have not been tampered with by breeders striving to make a particular genetic fashion statement. They require no surgery or inordinate molding to make them presentable. Again, breeders are full of accounts about how Pomeranians are able to differentiate between similar sounds—the step of his owner on the stairs as opposed to that of a stranger, or the sound of his owner's car door from the sound of all other car doors.

Smell and Taste

The sense of smell is another area where the Pomeranian seems to have lost none of his ancestral abilities. Scenting ability in the Pom, according to experienced dog people, seems to be on a par with his excellent eyesight and acute hearing. Hugo and some of his kindred have also done well in American Kennel Club (AKC) tracking tests!

Pomeranians have a reputation for being somewhat careful eaters. They seem to relish the taste of good-quality food while clearly rejecting more mundane fare. It would be unfair to call them picky about their food, but Poms do have definite likes and dislikes. A dog of any breed can be spoiled by inappropriate feeding practices that can lead to poor eating habits. With a dog as smart as the Pom,

---

CAUTION

Corporal Punishment

The Pomeranian is a dog of acute sensibilities; this is also true of his sense of touch. Corporal punishment may be felt by a Pom much more sharply than needed or intended, especially by a young dog. It is important to note that the Pomeranian can be negatively affected by all physical reprimanding. Small children or unthinking adults can do real damage, both physically and mentally, by striking a Pomeranian. *Don't hit any pets, but especially not a Pom!*

care must be taken to feed him high-quality dog food from the beginning and to make any dietetic changes gradually and only when absolutely necessary.

Pomeranians and other toy dog breeds have some dental difficulties with loose or displaced teeth. Many breeders and veterinarians suggest that consistently (read that to be *all* the time) feeding premium quality *dry* puppy and dog food is the wisest course of action for a Pom owner. The excellent dry food helps to clean and strengthen Hugo's teeth.

Touch

Although Poms may be somewhat reserved and guarded with strangers, once that stranger is acknowledged as a friend, the Pomeranian greatly enjoys physical contact, seeming to actually luxuriate in the touch of a favored human. This makes veterinary care easier with Pomeranians than with some breeds that seem to resent the human touch, especially from a human other than their owners. Some veterinarians assert that once a Pom knows and trusts a veterinarian, the dog often seems to readily accept the entire experience.

Meeting Other Dogs

As mentioned earlier, the Pomeranian is a brave and intelligent little dog. The accent here must certainly emphasize *little*. Hugo doesn't know he is a member of a breed of one of the smallest dogs on earth. He may believe that he is Buck from the *Call of the Wild*. In Hugo's mind it may seem perfectly logical that he could attack much larger dogs. It is crucial that a little dog's owner recognize the imminent and actual danger if such a confrontation

presents. Pom owners sometimes must save the Pomeranian from his own natural impulses.

As with small children and Pomeranians, a larger, stronger dog, perhaps not even meaning any damage, can seriously injure a 5- or 6-pound (2.3–2.7-kg) Pom. All reasonable care must be taken to lessen the chances of this occurring. Under normal circumstances, the Pomeranian can meet and interact with other dogs without much potential jeopardy. There are always situations, however, and the Pom may not always be able *or willing* to avoid trouble.

Hugo's bristling and bustling confidence may be enough to discourage hostility in a well-behaved larger dog. Nevertheless, not every larger dog that a Pom can possibly encounter will be well behaved. With dogs of his own

CAUTION

The Pom as Pugilist

The Pomeranian often has a "superiority complex" and doesn't realize he is a member of one of the smallest of dog breeds. Pom owners should keep their often feisty, little pets out of conflicts with other dogs, be they Poodles, Rottweilers, or Great Danes.

relative size, the Pomeranian is quite capable of maintaining his own sense of decorum. It is interesting to note that Poms in a multidog, multibreed household generally serve as peace-makers rather than instigators. Several Pomeranians in a home quickly work out their own accommodations and arrangements with sled dog-like efficiency and effectiveness.

AKC Standard

General Appearance: The Pomeranian is a compact, short-backed, active toy dog. He has a soft, dense undercoat with a profuse harsh-textured outer coat. His heavily plumed tail is set high and lies flat on his back. He is alert in character, exhibits intelligence in expression, is buoyant in deportment, and is inquisitive by nature. The Pomeranian is cocky, commanding, and animated as he gaits. He is sound in composition and action.

Size, Proportion, Substance: The average weight of the Pomeranian is from three to seven pounds, with the ideal weight for the show specimen being four to six pounds. Any dog over or under the limits is objectionable.

However, overall quality is to be favored over size. The distance from the point of shoulder to the point of buttocks is slightly shorter than from the highest point of the withers to the ground, the distance from the brisket to the ground is half the height at the withers. He is medium-boned, and the length of his legs is in proportion to a well-balanced frame. When examined, he feels sturdy.

Head: The *head* is in balance with the body. The *muzzle* is rather short, straight, fine, free of lippiness and never snipey. His *expression* is alert and may be referred to as fox-like. The *skull* is closed. The top of the skull is slightly rounded, but not domed. When viewed from the front and side, one sees small *ears* which are mounted high and carried erect. To form a wedge, visualize a line from the tip of the nose ascending through the center of the eyes and the tip of the ears. The *eyes* are dark, bright, medium in size and almond-shaped. They are set well into the skull on either side of a well-pronounced stop. The pigment is black on the nose and eye rims except self-colored in brown, beaver, and blue dogs. The *teeth* meet in a scissors bite. One tooth out of alignment is acceptable.

Major Faults: Round, domed skull; undershot mouth; overshot mouth.

Neck, Topline, Body: The *neck* is short with its base set well into the shoulders to allow the head to be carried high. The *back* is short with a level *topline*. The *body* is compact and well-ribbed with brisket reaching the elbow. The plumed *tail* is one of the characteristics of the breed, and lies flat and straight on the back.

Forequarters: The Pomeranian has sufficient layback of shoulders to carry the neck and head proud and high. The *shoulders* are moderately muscled. The length of the shoulder blade and upper arm are equal. The *forelegs* are straight and parallel to each other. Height from elbows to withers approximately equals height from ground to elbow. The pasterns are straight and strong. The *feet* are well-arched, compact, and turn neither in nor out. He stands well up on his toes. *Dewclaws* may be removed.

Major Faults: Down in pasterns.

Hindquarters: The angulation of the hindquarters balances that of the forequarters. The buttocks are well behind the set of the tail. The thighs are moderately muscled with *stifles* that are moderately bent and clearly defined. The hocks are perpendicular to the ground and the *legs* are straight and parallel to each other. The *feet* are well-arched, compact, and turn neither in nor out. He stands well up on his toes. *Dewclaws,* if any on the hind legs, may be removed.

Underneath the impressive coat of the Pomeranian is a short-bodied but muscular little dog. The muscle structure of the Pom clearly reveals the miniature sled dog physique.

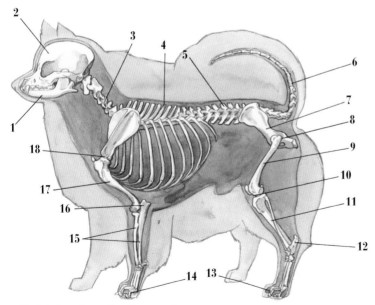

1. lower jaw (mandible)
2. skull (cranium)
3. cervical vertebrae
4. thoracic vertebrae
5. lumbar vertebrae
6. tail vertebrae
7. pelvis
8. hip joint
9. femur
10. knee joint (stifle)
11. tibia and fibula
12. hock (tarsas)
13. metatarsals
14. metacarpals
15. radius and ulna
16. elbow
17. humerus
18. shoulder joint

Skeletal system of a Pomeranian

Major Faults: Cowhocks or lack of soundness in hind legs or stifles.

Gait: The Pomeranian's gait is smooth, free, balanced and vigorous. He has good reach in his forequarters and strong drive with his hindquarters. Each rear leg moves in line with the foreleg on the same side. To achieve balance, his legs converge slightly inward toward a center line beneath his body. The rear and front legs are thrown neither in nor out. The topline remains level, and his overall balance is maintained.

Coat: A Pomeranian is noted for its double coat. The *undercoat* is soft and dense. The *outercoat* is long, straight, glistening and harsh in texture. A thick undercoat will hold up and permit the guard hair to stand off from the Pomeranian's body. The coat is abundant from the neck and fore part of the shoulders and chest, forming a frill which extends over the shoulders and chest. The head and leg coat is tightly packed and shorter in length than that of the body. The forequarters are well-feathered to the hock. The tail is profusely covered with long, harsh, spreading straight hair. Trimming for neatness and a clean outline is permissible.

Major Faults: Soft, flat or open coat.

Color: All colors, patterns and variations thereof are allowed and must be judged on an equal basis. *Patterns: Black and Tan*—tan or rust sharply defined, appearing above each eye and on muzzle, throat, and forechest, on all legs and feet and below the tail. The richer the tan the more desirable; *Brindle*—the base color

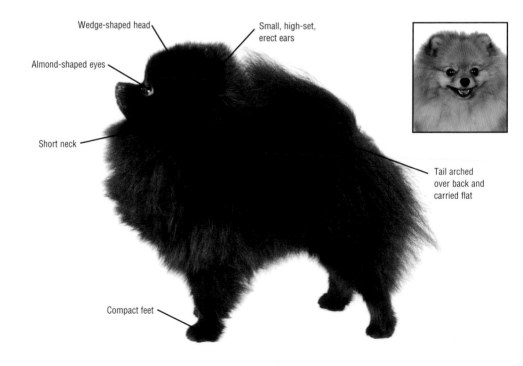

Wedge-shaped head

Small, high-set, erect ears

Almond-shaped eyes

Short neck

Tail arched over back and carried flat

Compact feet

TIP

Understanding the Standard

The AKC Standard for the Pomeranian is a written description of what the perfect Pomeranian should look like, move like, and act like. The terms and word-pictures represent the best of many decades of thought and discussion by the foremost breeders, judges, and experts on this breed. People new to the dog world in general and the Pomeranian world specifically, may not completely understand all the points engendered in this collective wisdom of all these Pomeranian breed-scholars. It is recommended that you visit a number of dog shows and find several experienced and highly reputable Pom people to discuss with you the nuances and phraseology of this Standard.

is gold, red, or orange-brindled with strong black cross stripes; *Parti-color*—is white with any other color distributed in patches with a white blaze preferred on the head. *Classifications:* The Open Classes at specialty shows may be divided by color as follows: Open Red, Orange, Cream, and Sable; Open Black, Brown, and Blue; Open Any Other Color, Pattern, or Variation.

Temperament: The Pomeranian is an extrovert, exhibiting great intelligence and a vivacious spirit, making him a great companion dog as well as a competitive show dog. *Even though a toy dog, the Pomeranian must be subject to the same requirements of sound-*

Author's Note
About the Merle Color Pattern

At the time of this writing, there is a great deal of controversy, pro and con, about the merle color pattern. The American Pomeranian Club membership is expected to vote on this color pattern issue in the near future.

ness and structure prescribed for all breeds, and any deviation from the ideal described in the standard should be penalized to the extent of the deviation.

Approved December 9, 1996
Effective January 31, 1997

CONSIDERATIONS BEFORE A POM BECOMES YOUR PET

There are some basic questions that you should honestly answer before you go a step further toward Pom ownership. If a Pomeranian is to be a sometime pet, a fashion accessory, or something to make you look cool, FORGET ABOUT IT! If you want a perpetual puppy that will always be a cute and tiny munchkin of about eight weeks old, Grow up! If you want a canine companion that never sheds, never leaves a puddle or a pile in an inappropriate place, clean up your erroneous thinking and get a photo of a Pom instead!

Are You Ready?

Pomeranians are living, breathing, loving pets that will have all the bodily functions of other dogs. Poms will go through the same age phases that other dogs do, and on anyone's absolute perfection meter will fail to reach 100 percent, as with all other pets—and people. A realistic look at your lifestyle, your expectations, and yourself is essential *before* you bring a Pomeranian into your home. Realistically gauge yourself on these questions and you'll have a better vision about owning a Pom.

✔ Does *each* person in your home know and understand what having a Pom will mean and entail?
✔ Does *each* person in your home willingly accept this role and his or her responsibilities?
✔ Is each person enthusiastic about sharing time and attention with a new pet?
✔ Does your family, as a group, have enough quality time to bring in a new family member?
✔ Does your family have the financial resources to undertake a long-term relationship with a pet that will rely on you totally?

✔ Does your family have the maturity and emotional stability to act appropriately if, at first, your Pom barks too much, chews up valuable things, and causes messes on carpets and floors?

✔ Do you and your family want a commitment that brings an emotional price tag if your new pet should become injured, ill, or even die?

✔ Is your family willing to enlist others, such as veterinarians, trainers, and Pom breeders, to solve problems that may confront your pet?

✔ Is your family more interested in just owning a dog than gaining a new, and admittedly furry, family member?

When answering these questions, remember that for you, a failure will mean returning a dog to his breeder, finding your dog a new home, or even taking this Pom to the animal shelter. For the Pomeranian you thought you wanted however, leaving you will mean being rejected by the humans he has come to worship and adore. Even if Pomeranians—or just this particular Pom—don't fit in with your family, this pet now faces an unhappy and uncertain future. Helping you to avoid this—for you and the Pomeranian—is reason enough for these personal questions. Do yourself and your potential Pomeranian pet a big favor, and answer them as honestly as possible.

Puppy or Adult?

Part of the answer to the age of the Pom you obtain hinges on what end purpose you have in mind for the dog. Obedience work,

Agility, or a dog show career can usually be best accomplished by purchasing a puppy from appropriate breeding stock and working with that puppy as he grows up. As companions, there may very well be adult Pomeranians available. You can check with Pomeranian rescue groups, highly reputable Pom breeders (*no puppy mills, impulse puppy sellers of "teacup" breeders need apply*) from contact with the American Pomeranian Club (see page 92 for address).

Bringing a puppy into your home is much like bringing a human baby into your home. This little girl Pom, Prissy, is a totally dependent entity that will need much care, love, and supervision. Like a human baby, Prissy will make messes, cry in the middle of the night, and require a lot of attention. She will need to be handled gently and given the first, rudimentary steps in becoming a well-trained adult Pomeranian.

Some adult (or older teen) responsible person should help the Pom puppy adjust to her new home. This will require time and effort. Be certain that this person wants to do this crucial job and is able to successfully do it. This role might require a few days of vacation time away from work to help Prissy settle in.

Prissy will need consistent care, without fail, as the highest priority. Perhaps the cavalryman in the Old West, who could not eat or rest until he had taken care of his horse, sets a good example for caring dog owners. A puppy or an older dog should receive attention before any other activity. You brought her here; she didn't come uninvited.

An older (or rescued) Pomeranian may not need as much immediate attention or supervision as a puppy, but even a well-trained adult

---

================ T I P ================

Male or Female

Both male and female Pomeranians make wonderful pets and can have sparkling careers in the Obedience or show ring. Females are affectionate, clearly feminine, and often become very attached to their families (as do males). Prissy or Hugo should do equally well within a well-prepared, Pom-knowledgeable and caring home and family.

---

dog will need some adjustment time in a new home. An older dog or rescued Pom may even have a particular set of problem dynamics. She may have been mistreated and, as a result, be snappish and defensive. She may have been closely attached to someone in her previous home and may grieve, sometimes even to the point of risking ill health. Prissy, as an adopted adult, may have learned another lifestyle and have some difficulty adjusting to yours. There are any number of problems that can and do arise, but an aware and thoughtful new Pomeranian owner can find a way to resolve most of them. Remember that Pomeranians are famous for their adaptability!

If you are a first-time dog owner or a *new-to-Poms person*, perhaps the best route to take would be to start a regimen of study. Books, Pomeranian breeders, veterinarians, and other dog professionals can help you avoid major pitfalls, but only if you will listen and then apply what you have learned.

Spaying and Neutering

If you choose a female and showing is not your goal, have her spayed. All the problems that can stem from your female coming "in season" will be eliminated. However, spaying will keep her from being eligible for entry in a dog show. Males can also be neutered, which will not affect their pet quality and will actually make them more tractable if they should come into contact with unspayed females. Spayed females and neutered males can still compete in many other sanctioned Pom activities (Obedience, Agility, Rally, Herding, Tracking, and so forth).

Male Aggression

A male Pom is 100 percent male in spite of his small size. He will have a tendency to mark his territory by hiking his leg and urinating on walks and outings. A male can show aggressive behavior when confronted with strange dogs, but good training and good supervision on your part can prevent any potentially dangerous confrontations with larger dogs. It is wise to remember that the male Pomeranian may not always realize that he is much smaller than some adversaries. As with small children, larger dogs can do severe damage to a Pomeranian. Even a playful puppy of a larger breed could hurt your Pomeranian. Guard against this by being alert to any situation where such a tragedy could occur.

Note: When bringing a Pom into a home where there is a cat, the same sort of preventive care must be undertaken. Some cats are much larger than any Pomeranian. With his prominent eyes and inquisitive nature, a Pom, especially a youngster, could sustain an eye injury from a well-aimed paw by a disgruntled feline.

Pet or Show Quality?

It is important to decide whether you want a pet-quality puppy or a show-quality puppy. "Pet quality" should never be a catchall phrase for reject puppies any more than "show quality" automatically guarantees you a top show dog in the future.

Pet-quality puppies may be excellent Agility, Therapy, or Obedience dogs and can certainly excel as companions. As a rule, these puppies have some little (often unnoticeable) conformation flaws that make it impossible for them to be considered for the show ring. These flaws are generally cosmetic in form, such as being a little too large, and should not include any physical disabilities or conditions that would make or cause such a puppy to be unhealthy or unsound.

True show-quality puppies are much harder to locate. Some breeders are reluctant to sell a puppy with show potential to a first-time Pom owner or to an owner who may not be willing or financially able to allow the puppy to reach his full show potential. Show-quality puppies will be considerably more expensive than most pet-quality puppies, but if showing your Pom is your ultimate goal, study hard and buy the best possible puppy from the best possible stock. Occasionally, breeders will make arrangements that will allow a serious dog exhibitor to own a dog in partnership with the breeder. These arrangements, while not common for first-time Pomeranian buyers, do happen. They usually hinge on whether you possess the skill, motivation, and budget to give a show dog the best possible exposure and on whether you can convince a serious Pom breeder that you do.

Pet-quality puppies, though somewhat less expensive and generally more available than show-quality puppies, should be healthy, happy Poms quite capable of becoming a key part of your life. These pet puppies should never come from a puppy mill or a neglectful, ignorant backyard breeder. If showing is not in your game plan, a spayed or neutered pet-quality Pomeranian is obviously tailored precisely to fit your needs.

Selecting a Puppy

Before you begin the selection process, there are a number of things that will make your task easier and less of a gamble.

✔ Learn as much as you can about the Pomeranian breed.

✔ Contact the American Kennel Club and the American Pomeranian Club (see page 92 for addresses), regional breed clubs, and top (by undisputed reputation) breeders.

✔ Visit dog shows and chat with Pomeranian breeders-exhibitors there. Look at their show dogs. See what the breed is supposed to look like at its very best. In short, diligently get to know the Pom before you set out on your quest.

✔ Visually inspect as many Poms as possible and, if you seem to like a certain color, certainly take time to look at many dogs of that color. Remember, you are looking for a pet and if a good one of a different color becomes available, don't ignore him or her.

Show Quality

✔ If you are after a show-quality puppy, stick with top quality breeders who may help you find the puppy you are seeking. ABSOLUTELY forget about bargain basement, dealer-sold, puppy mill-originated, and backyard Poms that may come your way.

✔ Center your thinking not on one specific Pomeranian, but on a specific family or "line."

✔ Concentrate on the specific attributes you want such a puppy to possess.

✔ Find out which breeder has a top reputation—not just a top show record.

✔ Do a lot of questioning and listening and refrain from buying any puppy unless he fits the precise model you have thoughtfully constructed. Remember, even with the best breeder selling you the puppy of the highest possible potential, not every such situation produces a winning show dog.

To pick a show-quality puppy, you would do well to make friends with a Pom breeder who can help you best apply the written descriptions in the Pomeranian Breed Standard (see pages 16–19) to a young puppy. Finding the show puppy you are seeking may be a long, arduous process, but if showing is your knowledgeable and sincere goal, it is the only way you can go about it. While most nationally-recognized breeders are honest, helpful people, *"buyer beware"* is always a good motto when you are new in any interest area, including show dogs.

Pet Quality

Finding a pet-quality puppy may be much simpler, but can be as potentially risky. Just because you are planning to spend hundreds for a pet rather than thousands for a show puppy doesn't mean that you should not read, study, compare, check around, and try to find the best-quality puppy. Remember that we are talking about adding a family member that may be with you for a decade-and-a-half or more. Care is the watchword.

Your search for the right Pom should center on the absolutely best sources. Seek out highly reputable breeders whose reputation is based on the quality of the dogs and puppies they have to sell. Avoid the "fast food," impulsive, gambler approach to purchasing a pet; haste in buying the first Pomeranian you see may lead you and your family down a very bad and sad path. Impulsively picking a poor-quality Pom now may become a real problem for you both immediately and on down the line. You may have chosen the wrong breed, the wrong dog in the wrong breed, or the wrong dog in the wrong breed from the wrong source. You may be simply annoyed when a pet doesn't work out—the pet will be devastated. You can always find another dog, but if your unwanted pet bounces from owner to owner or ends up in an

══════ CAUTION ══════

How to Spot a Puppy Mill
- Puppy Mills are in dog breeding to make a profit, not to assure their customers the best possible puppy.
- Puppy Mills often have many litters at any one time with "whatever you want" as a sales mantra.
- Puppy Mills will want to meet you somewhere other than at their kennel location.
- Puppy Mills are more interested in your ability to pay than your potential as a good home for a puppy.
- Should you be able to visit a Puppy Mill, the smell and filth and bedraggled-looking dogs will often give it away.
- Puppy Mills often have elaborate websites with the promise to ship a Pomeranian puppy sight unseen.

animal shelter to face a very uncertain future, it is a very sad situation.

A pet-quality Pomeranian will often come from a breeder of show stock. Because many more pet-quality puppies than show puppies are born, you should be able to find a good puppy from this source. In this case, you have a chance to look at your puppy's environment. Ask to see the mother and father (if possible) of the puppy. Most breeders welcome potential pet-puppy buyers who will take the time to carefully check things out. They know these seekers are the ones most likely to give a puppy the care he deserves. Highly conscientious and well-respected dog breeders are concerned

about their reputations and are also faced with finding good homes for their excess pet-quality puppies. While you are looking for a place from which to obtain a good pet Pom puppy, they are looking for a good owner for one of their not-quite-show specimens. This can, and often does, work out for all three of you—the breeder, you, and especially the puppy.

Backyard breeders: You may be tempted to seek out the readily available "bargain basement" Pomeranian. If you can't afford to get a good Pom, you can't afford one at all! Classified ads and notes on a sell-and-swap bulletin board may be from decent, amateur Pom owners who have an extra puppy of good quality. But how will you know? The odds are over-

whelmingly against an inexperienced backyard breeder being able to sell a puppy of sufficient quality to an inexperienced Pom seeker.

You are definitely on your own when you choose a source that can't give you a real guarantee on the long-term health and temperament of any puppy you may want to buy. If you want a really good pet-quality puppy that can grow into a very good pet, start with top-quality show breeders who are striving for real quality. Their non-show or pet prospects may be more expensive than a Pomeranian from the bulletin board at the corner store or some other bargain source (but often not), but you stand an infinitely greater chance of getting what you really want—a good Pomeranian.

Breeders

"Diamonds in the rough" are tough, if not impossible, to find. Seek a potential show-quality puppy from a show-oriented breeder. An Obedience trial puppy probably should come from stock that has distinguished itself in the Obedience training. Decide what you want in the puppy and then go to the place you are most likely to find it.

To sum up, when choosing a Pom puppy, take time to observe the puppies. Don't ruin all the effort you have made up to this point by fixating on one puppy and making your ideal fit that puppy because she's there and so are you. Stick with your game plan and make every effort to determine if the puppies shown coincide with what you are seeking. Remember that you are seeking a sound, healthy puppy that will be a family member/companion for many years to come. If you act impulsively now, you will have a lot of time to regret it in the future.

Papers

Prior to actually choosing a puppy from any source, make sure you will receive three things:

1. The puppy's health records, showing dates of vaccination, deworming, and a health certificate, signed by a veterinarian stating that the puppy has been examined and appears healthy.

2. The American Kennel Club (AKC) registration certificate stating that your Pom is a purebred. With this certificate you should also receive application papers to send to the AKC to register the puppy in your name.

3. A pedigree, which is really only as good as the source from which the puppy comes, showing the puppy's parents and recent lineage.

These documents are very important and if they are not available, don't buy the puppy!

Making the Selection

Assuming that all the papers are in order and you feel that the source you have chosen will be reliable and will guarantee the puppy to be healthy and sound—always best to get this in writing—the time for selection is at hand. You already have an idea of what you want—male or female, color, quality, and so on—and hopefully you have chosen a source that will give you several puppies from which to choose. Pomeranians usually have very small litters—one, two, or maybe three puppies—so you may have to wait to get a puppy that fits color or other specific requirements that you and your family may have. Waiting for exactly the right puppy, after you have taken the time to really decide what kind of puppy that is, should be no real problem.

Carefully handle each puppy that fits your requirements, remembering that an eight-week-old puppy will not clearly reflect all that she may become. Depending on the amount of contact with outsiders the puppies have had, they may be somewhat apprehensive at your approach, but you can tell if they seem healthy and you can see if they appear sound and not overly frightened by your visit.

You may not find exactly what you are seeking, but don't be afraid to walk away. There are other puppies, and this is a long-term relationship that you are planning. If that special puppy is there, the one that is bold, bright-eyed, and fits your requirements, you may have found your new family member. The accent is on the word *may*. You want to refrain from mentally and emotionally deciding on the puppy until *your* veterinarian has had a chance to inspect her and pronounce her sound and healthy. Time taken now will be well worth it later, when this friendly puppy becomes the ideal companion that has been the object of all your reading, questioning, and searching.

Poms and Children

Pomeranians and very small children *absolutely* do not mix. This is not the dog's fault, but merely a realistic assertion that small children can seriously, sometimes even fatally, injure very small dogs. Little legs can easily

Picking Up a Puppy

If you are visiting several sources looking for a Pom puppy, always wash your hands with antibacterial soap or wipes between stops. It would be tragic to think that you were responsible for transmitting some disease to several litters of Pomeranian puppies.

The best way to handle a tiny Pom puppy is to gently pick her up, supporting the back and rear end with one hand and the chest with the other. The puppy will feel supported, more comfortable, and therefore safer. Always remember how fragile a tiny Pomeranian puppy is and do everything to keep the youngster from harm.

break with rough treatment and a little dog jumping from a child's arms can be all that it would take for the Pom to be hurt or killed. *Children must always be supervised when they are playing with a Pomeranian.*

Not even all older children are mature enough to be left unsupervised with a fragile Pomeranian puppy—or an adult Pom for that matter. Let common sense guide you in these matters. The safety of your pet should be your prime concern.

Expenses

A pet-quality Pom puppy should cost you hundreds of dollars while show puppies can cost thousands or more. (A puppy of a "rare, exotic" color from a puppy mill source may actually cost you more than a good puppy from a reputable breeder, both on the initial investment and in ongoing health expenses.) A reasonable pet ownership budget for veterinary care, premium pet food, occasional professional grooming visits and other items could average more than $50 per month. Good care at home will save you additional dollars.

"Teacup" Poms

The so-called "teacup" Pomeranian is a GIANT mistake! There is actually no such thing (according to *all* reputable dog breeders) as a "teacup Pomeranian," "toy Pomeranian," or "miniature Pomeranians." Don't buy one! Don't even accept one as a gift! These ultra-tiny Poms of 1 or 2 pounds (0.5–0.9 kg) may be cute, but they are almost always a huge veterinary bill—and a lot of heartache—a canine disaster waiting to happen. Extra-tiny puppies happen sometimes by accident, but keep away from someone, like most puppy mills, who intentionally breeds for these dwarf-Poms. Run away fast from these breed-for-greed types. People pushing these "teacup" dogs are probably into a scam that separates you from your money and provides you with a desperately short-lived puppy that will break your heart and possibly your bank account!

Christmas Puppies

This advice may fly in the face of tradition, your personal wishes, and several other accepted ideas, but surprising someone with a puppy on Christmas morning is a terrible idea! Bringing a new puppy into your home at a time when a lot of hectic activities are planned cannot help an already bewildered puppy adjust to a new environment. Instead, obtain the puppy several weeks before Christmas or several weeks after Christmas when she can be the center of attention, can get the care she needs and deserves, and can realize that these new people in her life really do love her. Never buy a puppy to surprise somebody! Puppies, Poms especially, deserve to be planned for and cared for.

CARING FOR YOUR POMERANIAN

Any change of environment can be stressful for any dog. For Hugo to have the best possible start in his new home, there are a number of things you can do to make the transition less traumatic.

Preparations

✔ Purchase a sturdy, flat-bottomed water bowl and a similar one for food. These should not easily turn over and yet should be shallow enough for your Pomeranian to be able to get *at* their contents without having to get *in* with the contents.

✔ Obtain some of the *exact* same food that the puppy has been eating. Change brands some other time, if you wish, but definitely not during such a trying time for your new dog.

✔ A dog crate or carrier (see the chapter "Training Your Pomeranian," page 79), perhaps of the airline-approved type, will be essential in fulfilling the "den" requirements so important to Pomeranians. This crate or carrier will be your dog's special place within your home. It will also be a great aid in house-training, as we shall soon see.

✔ Hugo will need a collar and lead of appropriate size—or perhaps a one-piece nylon collar and lead—to introduce him to the big, new world.

✔ You should also purchase a good-quality grooming comb and brush. Ask the breeder or a pet products store professional to recommend a good brand, specifying the tiny size of puppy Hugo.

Toys

A very important area where the breeder or pet products retailer may be able to assist is with toys. If your Pomeranian puppy has taken an interest in a particular toy while still at the breeder's, by all means obtain that particular toy. Pomeranians are great little possessors and such a toy would help the pup, or an older dog for that fact, adjust to his new home with you. If no such special interest in a particular toy has been observed, ask breeders, veterinarians, and other dog people about the kind of toys to get.

If you have chosen a puppy and are yet to take him home, you might even introduce a plaything to your chosen puppy at the breeder's before he is ready to go home so that it will already be familiar. Touch the toy with your bare hands and also have your family members handle the toy so that your scents will not be completely alien to the puppy when the time to go home with you arrives. In any case, toys are essential for Poms.

Another essential is the "puppy-proofing" that must be done before you bring your Pomeranian home. This can be an interesting and enlightening experience for you. In much the same way that you might prepare a room for an active toddler, you need to go over all the areas in your home to which the puppy will have access for anything that could do

CHECKLIST

Puppy Proofing Specifics

✔ You should look for coins, pins, needles, tacks, beads, toxic houseplants, or anything that a small, inquisitive puppy might discover and possibly chew or swallow.

✔ Also be on the lookout for exposed electrical wires or things that, if pulled on by a puppy, might fall on him.

✔ Check for exposed woodwork that, especially in older homes, may have lead-based paint or that may have been treated with some chemical polish or spray that might do harm to a young, teething puppy.

✔ Stairwells and narrow spaces behind appliances or furniture where a puppy might fall or get trapped are obvious danger areas.

✔ Pomeranian puppies don't need to be doing much jumping. Their little legs can so easily break on what might not appear to be any distance at all, as from the sofa to the floor. Damage can also be done to little shoulders, knees, and hips. Keep Hugo off the furniture for his sake and the furniture's.

him harm. More than one dog expert suggests that you actually get down on the floor and check out each room from the tiny puppy's perspective.

Young Hugo will have had limited experience outside of that gained through his mother, littermates, and his breeder. You will now have to ensure that this special puppy gets the right learning opportunities he needs to avoid injury through an oversight on your part or puppyish ignorance on his part.

Enlist all your family members in doing a safety check. Crawl all over the floor seeking potentially dangerous objects. Close off stairwells and other unsafe places. Be sure to purchase the things Hugo will need. Remind all members of the family that having a new puppy, literally underfoot, means new responsibilities. Go over a list of possible problems and the assigned duties of each family member.

Now you and your puppy's breeder must work out a time that will be the very best for the puppy to go home with you. Arrange to be home for the first several days, or have a responsible person at home to help the puppy adjust. You are now ready to bring your Pom puppy home.

Adjustment Period

The Crate

As mentioned earlier, an important way to help your new Pomeranian adjust to his new home is by purchasing a dog crate or carrier. As with toys, you might also introduce your new puppy to this new crate or carrier even *before* you bring him home. By taking this preliminary step, the puppy, or even an older dog, can have his own den with its own familiar scents and comforting sameness before he ever arrives at your home.

The importance of such a den for Hugo cannot be overestimated.

T I P

Good Toys for Poms

Pet products retailers often have loads of wonderful toys for your Pomeranian. Try to find toys that won't splinter or come apart after a lengthy period of hard chewing. Remember to keep Pom toys small, but tough. One pet expert recommends thoroughly clean (and undamaged) golf balls smeared with peanut butter, which is then wiped off leaving only the aroma to attract your Pom's attention.

It will be his own special place of rest, peace, and sanctuary, within your home. Such a place of warmth and safety will be crucial to your puppy's emotional and physical well-being. Some humans mistakenly see using a crate

as locking *in* the dog, but the Pomeranian sees it as a way to lock the people *out!* In the trying times of adjusting to his new home, this den is a safe haven in a world that Hugo may frankly find confusing or even frightening.

There are some steps you can take to make it a little easier on the puppy *within* the crate.

✔ An old-fashioned hot water bottle (non-leaking, of course) or some toy or piece of familiar bedding can be comforting to the puppy.

✔ An old wind-up alarm clock, whose ticking may serve to replace the mother's heartbeat, can also be an aid; make sure the alarm portion of this clock is inoperable.

✔ You might turn on a radio (safely away from the actual crate) on low volume to an all-night talk station so it can be a human-voice comfort to the puppy in falling asleep. For tips on crate training, see page 91.

The Ride Home

For an eight-week-old puppy, the actual trip to his new home can be traumatic in itself. If possible, have a member of the family, seated and safely belted-in, in the backseat gently hold the puppy. Be sure to have this family member support Hugo's body from beneath while not squeezing him too tightly. During the ride, an old bathrobe and towels might not be a bad idea in the event of motion sickness. If this family member could already be an "old friend," from previous visits to the puppy, so much the better. Poms do love to travel, but even a short car ride may be overwhelming to a very young Pom. Don't get things off to a bad start.

If the journey is several hours or more, frequent stopping for "nature breaks" and to reassure the puppy are a good idea. If the puppy cannot be in someone's arms, he should be in his carrier. Don't allow the puppy to stand up or to attempt to run around inside the car. Unexpected stops, sharp turns, or even falling off the car seat can cause injury, often serious injury.

Beginning Housetraining

Housetraining should begin prior to your Pomeranian puppy arriving at your home. If at all possible, choose an outside site that can be set aside as *THE PLACE* for the youngster to eliminate wastes. While paper training (training a puppy to relieve himself on newspapers somewhere inside the home) works, outside housetraining is preferable for many pet owners.

Remember that canines are, by nature, scenting creatures. They get much of their information (and subsequently their learning) from the smells they encounter. *THE PLACE* should become a primary elimination location after your Pomeranian has marked it with his own urine and feces. Each time you return Hugo to *THE PLACE*, he will catch his own scent there and understand what this spot is for and relieve himself there.

When you arrive home, give Hugo a chance to nose around in the outside area where you will normally be walking and where you will want him to defecate and urinate. Training begins *now* by not confusing the puppy about where you expect him to urinate and defecate. When Hugo relieves himself in the appropriate area, pet and praise him liberally. Pomeranians are smart and it shouldn't take too long for him to associate going outside with this

specific location for urination and defecation. This type of patience and consistency on your part will make housetraining much less of a trauma for both Hugo and you.

Exploring

Assuming you have puppy-proofed all the areas inside your home where Hugo will be allowed to enter, give your new family member some time to explore. Remember that he is still just a puppy and may tire quickly. Certainly play with him, but when Hugo shows signs of tiring, return him to his den-crate. Hugo will soon learn where he is to sleep and may even

soon begin to go directly there when he is tired or simply seeks the comfort of his own place.

Allowing the Puppy to Adjust

Hugo will now have to learn to adjust to being alone, without his mother or his littermates, but *you* will also have to make an adjustment. You are training your Pomeranian by your actions, and rapid learning is taking place in his fertile mind. If you are intent on crate-training your puppy—using the crate or carrier to serve as Hugo's home-within-the-home—then you must let him know that he will not be allowed out, cuddled, petted, or fawned over when he whines or cries. You can quietly speak to him to reassure him that you are there, but if you (or any other member of your household) do take Hugo into your arms when he whimpers or cries, he will soon learn exactly how to get into your arms— simply by crying.

Consistency is vital here. If you are determined, as you certainly should be, not to give in to the wails and plaintive puppy noises, and some other family member slips in and takes the puppy out of his sleeping place, then all of your resolve is for nothing. No one prefers to listen to a sad, lonely puppy crying, but that puppy can become a sad, lonely *adult* dog that is still crying *if* consistent training is not firmly followed. Steel yourself and your family to a few nights of crying with the knowledge that, as with inoculations for disease, a little discomfort now will mean a much happier and better adjusted pet later.

Feeding the New Puppy

Feeding Hugo should not be too difficult, but again, consistency is important. You have already obtained *the very same* food that he has been eating. Using this same food, if the breeder was not experiencing some food-related problem with this puppy, on the same schedule to which the puppy is accustomed, will aid in avoiding some of the transitional stress. Even with the same diet, transplanting a puppy to a new home will have some negative impact on him. Expect some minor diarrhea for a day or so; see your veterinarian if it continues for more than a couple of days, especially when feeding the same diet. Keep on schedule

with your puppy's feedings. As with a human infant, much of the Hugo's first days will be taken up with eating and sleeping. If he is to adapt to his new environment quickly and easily, Hugo will need consistency. You and your family *must* be the source of that consistency.

Traveling with Your Pom

Traveling with a Pom is a good deal easier than with some breeds. The Pomeranian is a highly adaptable little dog that enjoys traveling and seems to suffer few side effects from it. Where some dogs are stressed by a change of scenery, the Pom takes it in stride and seems to thrive on it.

There are those Pomeranian breeders who believe that the Pomeranian's good record as a show dog and as an Obedience trial dog comes, at least in part, from his ability to do well in varied environments—his adaptability. Whether the Pom does well in competition on the road because he likes to travel is open to discussion. One thing is for sure: The Pomeranian can make a very good traveling buddy.

Traveling with any pet, even a good traveler like the Pomeranian, calls for some planning and preparations on your part. Since most Poms are crate-trained in a fiberglass carrier and can take their den with them, including your dog on your vacation could be a great idea.

Car Travel

You will make many trips of varying lengths with your Pomeranian in a private automobile. While the requirements for taking your dog with you on a longer trip in your car are not as stringent as those of an airline, you would still

CAUTION

Air Travel

Because of increasing and rapidly evolving restrictions on air travel, with and without pets, the wise Pom owner-traveler may want to contact the American Pomeranian Club or the American Kennel Club about their most current suggestions and recommendations about taking Hugo with you when you fly commercially.

do well not to take these extended car travel precautions too lightly.

1. Always have your Pomeranian in a carrier or in a doggy safety harness when you are riding together.

2. Check with the veterinarian for some motion sickness medications; don't feed Hugo in the immediate hours (five or six hours in advance) before you plan an extended motor trip, and provide him water only up to two hours before leaving.

3. Stop every hour or so to give the dog a breather, a drink of water, and some exercise.

4. Always use Hugo's leash and collar when you take him out of the carrier.

5. *NEVER* leave your dog in a parked car, even with windows rolled down, during the day when the temperature is as high as 60°F (16°C) (see "Heatstroke," page 74).

6. If you are traveling across country, check with auto clubs and travel guides about which motels and hotels allow pets in their rooms. When you make reservations by phone, you

might also confirm that they allow well-behaved pets. A little planning will make the trip safer and saner.

7. Avoid "pet walks" at rest areas if you have a very young puppy that could pick up a communicable disease from such a location. Go to a grassy area, out of regular walking traffic, at gas stations or other stops (other than rest areas). Always carry a "poop-bag" or similar item with you to clean up after Hugo.

Boarding Your Pom

If you can't take Hugo with you on your trip, boarding him may be one alternative. This is not as bleak a prospect as you might think. There are several good possibilities.

✔ In many locales, pet sitters are available to take care of your pet *in your own home* while you are away. Usually these are skillful, caring, bonded people who can furnish numerous valid references.

✔ You and Hugo may have a friend, neighbor, or family member who can care for your pet. He might be able to continue to stay in your home under this arrangement. This surrogate needs to be someone Hugo likes and who can give him the care he needs while you are away.

✔ Hugo's veterinarian or professional groomer may board dogs and would be already known and accepted by your Pomeranian in a place he knows.

✔ The responsible and reputable breeder from whom you bought Hugo, if located nearby, may be willing to take an alumnus in as a boarder, in which circumstance you will be absolutely sure of good care.

✔ There are some excellent boarding kennels that are accredited with the American Boarding Kennel Association (ABKA) (see page 92).

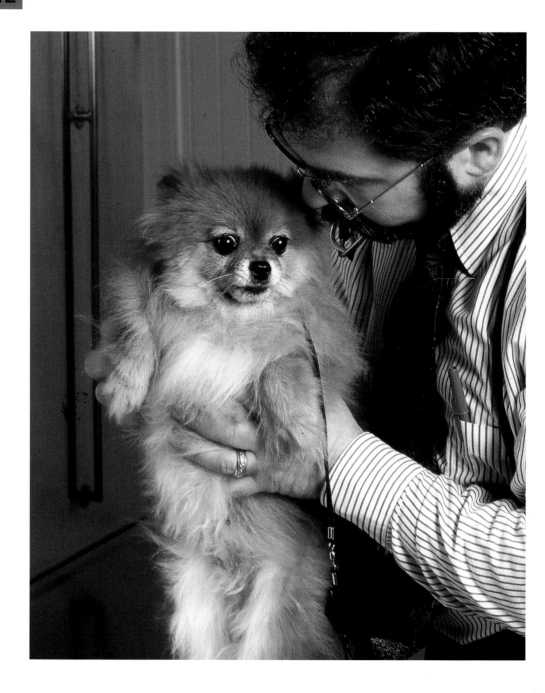

Protecting Your Pom

Protecting Hugo from diseases and accidental injury is one thing, but keeping him safe from thieves or from loss is quite another. Being able to identify your Pomeranian is more of a mindset than a list of "to do's." This mindset realizes that even with all his human-like expressions and affection, Hugo is still just a dog. As a dog, he can become the victim of straying away, being stolen, or becoming hopelessly lost on a trip.

Being able to effectively identify your pet is just as important as having his shot record up-to-date or having him ride safely in his crate on car trips. License tags affixed to a collar are required by law in many places, but these do not offer quick identification of a wayward Pom. Additionally, collars can come off (or be intentionally removed by dog thieves!). Even collars with your name and address are not always the ultimate safeguard for Hugo's safe identification.

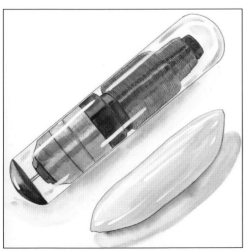

A microchip as compared to a grain of rice.

Tattooing

Some breeds, especially larger dogs, are tattooed with a number that can lead to the safe return of a missing dog. The identifying tattoos are often placed on the inner flank or inner upper thigh. Tattooing is still an effective way of permanently marking Hugo, but an easier and better way in the minds of many Pom owners is available.

Microchipping

A microchip, about the size of a grain of rice, is injected just under the skin between Hugo's shoulder blades. This is a lifelong identity source for your Pomeranian. Veterinarians and most animal shelters have digital scanners which can read the information encrypted on this microchip and help Hugo get home.

For a small fee national registries record your dog's information and make it available to the vet clinics or animal shelters scanning the chips. (This is also true of tattoos, if that form of pet ID is your preference.)

Microchips have greatly enhanced the safe return of lost, strayed, and stolen dogs of all types. This is just another way of expressing your love for Hugo and ensuring his eventual return if something separates the two of you. With a small and nearly painless injection and a registration fee, your pet and his important information is cataloged for life.

FEEDING YOUR POMERANIAN

You have gone to considerable effort to learn about and obtain a good-quality Pomeranian. What you feed Prissy will be a major factor in her health, both mental and physical, and in her longevity. The importance of a balanced diet and your understanding of what makes it balanced will be a key to this important part of dog ownership.

A Balanced Diet

The computer phrase "garbage in, garbage out" is also an apt point to remember about canine nutrition. Your Pomeranian will need a balanced diet to grow strong and healthy, and to develop the potential that is her genetic birthright. A poor diet can cause Prissy (or Hugo) a wide variety of medical, behavioral, and developmental problems. Avoiding a poor diet and establishing a solid nutritional plan isn't difficult. There are three basic rules:

1. provide your Pomeranian with a high-quality dog food,

2. avoid human food and table scraps,

3. *don't overfeed.*

Basic Nutrition

There are seven components to a balanced diet for your Pomeranian: proteins, carbohydrates, fats, vitamins, minerals, water, and consistency/knowledge.

Protein

Protein provides the dog with amino acids that are essential for growth, the maintenance of healthy muscle and bone, the repair of that same muscle and bone, the production of infection-fighting antibodies, and the production of hormones and enzymes that aid in the dog's body's chemical processes. Good sources of protein are meat and poultry products, milk products, fish meal, and corn.

Carbohydrates

Carbohydrates provide energy to power the Pom's internal motor. Thoroughly cooked grains, starches, and vegetables provide most of the carbohydrates seen in quality dog foods. Carbohydrates are measured in calories (as are fats and proteins).

Fats

Fat is another much more concentrated source of energy for your Pomeranian, which can provide more than twice as much energy as a like amount of protein or carbohydrates. Fat also provides the "delivery system" for the fat-soluble vitamins, A, D, E, and K, into your Pom's system for healthy skin and coat. In

addition, fat aids in maintaining a healthy nervous system and makes dog food taste better.

Vitamins

Vitamins are needed for general body functions and are needed in small quantities that are easily provided in a balanced diet of a high-quality dog food so that additional supplementation is *not* usually needed. The best source of vitamins is a well-balanced diet.

Minerals

Minerals are essential for normal body functioning; calcium and phosphorus are needed for strong bones, muscles, and teeth; potassium and sodium aid in the maintenance of a healthy nervous system and in the maintenance of normal bodily fluids; iron promotes healthy blood in your pet by transporting oxygen throughout its body.

Important note: A high-quality dog food will contain the appropriate levels of both vitamins and minerals. Don't try to supplement a high-quality dog food without first consulting your veterinarian. Both vitamins and minerals can easily be overdone.

Water

Water is often the most neglected part of a dog's diet, yet it is a very important component. Prissy will need plenty of clean, fresh water all the time. It might not hurt—you or your dog—if you had your water tested annually even if you are part of a municipal water system. With water purity a question in many communities, your actions here may be a good preventive against chemical imbalances or interactions.

Consistency/Knowledge

Another often-ignored aspect of a balanced diet is the manner in which you provide food to your dog. As in so many other areas of Pom care, consistency is important in diet as well. Find a high-quality dog food that your pet likes and stay with it. Even experienced dog people, who should know better, often buy one type of food, then they switch to another type, without regard for the dog's needs. Changing from one food source to another should usually take two weeks or longer with the gradual mixing of the new food with the old in ever-increasing amounts until the old is gone.

Your knowledge about canine nutrition and about dog foods is very important to the health of your Pomeranian, who has to depend on you.

Commercial Dog Food

There are a number of excellent high-quality dog foods on the market today, and an even greater number of inferior products trying to capture your attention and dog food dollars. As with finding the right Pomeranian for you, the adage "You get what you pay for" relates just as well to dog food. If you will take time to learn some basic facts about dog foods, you'll ultimately save money while providing a high-quality, balanced diet for your Pom. Prissy's veterinarian, her breeder, or her professional groomer may have information about which brands of high-quality dog food have done well for other Pomeranians and their owners and could work for you and Prissy.

You could find a pet food company that will let you talk to a pet nutritionist or staff veterinarian. Ask questions about the food and

about any Pomeranian test information they may have. The better companies have toll-free numbers and websites. These companies welcome questions and have skillful staff members available to help you with your dog food questions.

Dry Food

There are a number of advantages to a high-quality dry dog food. Most important, there are several dry foods that can truthfully call themselves "nutritionally complete." As such they will be the balanced diet you are seeking. Also, a quality dry dog food will help clean your dog's teeth and gums. Dry dog food is the most economical way to feed a premium dog food. It is easy to feed, easy to store, with no refrigeration needed to keep it fresh. Premium dry

Homemade Diets

Unless you are a trained animal nutritionist with access to all the products, vitamins, minerals, and other aspects that will be needed for a balanced diet, this approach is best left alone. Your Pom will need a complete nutrition program and such a program is available in high-quality dog food from several companies that have spent multimillions of dollars to make it available to you for Prissy. Home cooking is not only unnecessary, but it is hardly ever a good idea for the average Pomeranian owner.

dog foods are high in palatability and digestibility, producing smaller and firmer stools. Your dog actually eats less and gets more from a premium food. Dry dog food has about 10 percent moisture, so be certain you keep plenty of clean, fresh water available to your Pom. Also, remember to feed a dry food that is small enough for your Pom to easily eat.

It is important to remember that Pomeranians may have dental difficulties that can be greatly aided by feeding dry food that helps exercise teeth and gums. Dry food also promotes cleaner teeth and firmer bowel movements.

Treats

Leave table scraps off your Pomeranian's menu. If you don't start the habit of feeding the dog items from your plate, begging can be avoided. Also, table scraps aren't part of your goal—a nutritionally complete and balanced diet. A dog will often neglect her regular food in favor of treats and scraps.

There are some excellent dog biscuits available that are nutritionally complete and have the added bonus of helping to clean your dog's teeth and gums and give her a nutritional "chew" at the same time. Note that treats need to be apportioned with care lest they unbalance the balanced diet that you are trying to maintain.

If you feed a high-quality dry dog food, there is one trick you can use to give your pet a treat and some variety without throwing off the balanced diet. Put a small amount of your

Pom's dry food in a microwave-safe bowl. Add a teaspoon or two of water to the dry food. Microwave on High for about 30 seconds and allow the food to cool. The nutrients remain the same, but the fats in the dry food are pulled toward the surface. This will give the Pom the same food with a little different taste, not unlike the difference in a charcoal-broiled hamburger and one cooked on the stove. Don't use too much water on the dry dog food or you'll interfere with stool firmness. This method, with a little more water, is helpful in feeding older dogs with teeth problems where a softer diet is needed.

Feeding Requirements

Puppies

In order to get puppy Prissy off to the best possible start, for the first year of her life you will need a nutritionally complete balanced diet designed specifically for the needs of growing puppies. Puppies generally need *twice* as much in the way of nutrition than do adult dogs. Feed her the best high-quality puppy food available and you shouldn't run into any problems.

The key is to start your Pom puppy on the right nutritional diet from the very beginning. Try to find a high-quality puppy diet, if you are changing, in a size that will be easily handled by small-breed puppy such as the Pomeranian. Several premium dry foods fit this requirement. A puppy under six months old should be fed three or four times daily. At six months, cut back to two or three times daily, depending on the individual needs of the dog.

Adult Dogs

When your Pomeranian reaches physical maturity at around one year, her nutritional needs will change from those of a growing puppy into those of an adult. Two feedings per day will generally suffice as your Pom achieves her mature weight. Other than with added activities such as showing, Agility, or Obedience work, your Pom's nutritional needs should remain fairly constant for the next six or seven years. Of course, spaying or neutering your pet

can change the nutritional requirements to more like those of an older dog.

Older Dogs

When your Pom gets older, her metabolic rate will slow down and she will need somewhat less energy, and thus less fat and protein. It is important that the older Pomeranian of eight years or more not gain too much weight. This is also true of the spayed and neutered Pom even before she has reached eight years of age.

One of the hardest things to convince dog owners of is that an older dog doesn't need the same amount of food she did when she was

━━━ TIP ━━━

Food and Health Indicators

The food bowl is a good health indicator. Pay attention to the dog's eating habits. You may get an early warning to some ailment or physical condition that needs your veterinarian's attention. Also pay attention to the dog's bowel movements, another good health indicator.

younger. "But Prissy always gets two cups of dog food" is the commonly heard reply when food reduction is suggested. Prissy's owner is *not* helping her live a long and healthy life by continuing to feed her the same amount she ate when she was much younger.

Many of the premium dog foods now have foods designed for the less active metabolism of older dogs or for spayed and neutered dogs. Contact your veterinarian or the company that makes the dog food you have been using. (This would be a good time to take advantage of the 800 number or website of your premium dog food company.)

A Feeding Trial

Finding a balanced diet for your Pomeranian that she likes isn't that difficult. Perhaps you can find a veterinarian who has taken a special interest in canine nutrition. Become a label reader and ask lots of questions of the dog food companies. An aware consumer is a good consumer and your efforts will pay off for you and Prissy.

Always consult with your veterinarian on special dietetic problems that afflict some dogs; however, a good balanced diet program from puppyhood on should help your Pom avoid many ailments. Find a high-quality food and stick with it. If the product isn't doing what you think it should, follow this simple feeding trial below.

═CHECKLIST═

Feeding Trial
✔ Always compare apples to apples. Don't put a canned or semimoist food up against a dry food, for example.
✔ Buy a sample of a new food that you believe might give you the results you desire. Put it in a dog dish near your pet's regular food bowl. If the dog shows interest in the new food, let her eat an amount that is the equivalent of the regular amount you normally feed. Your dog may eat some of each or spurn the new food altogether. Don't let a piggish Pom eat more than she should regularly have.
✔ If your dog likes the new food, follow the gradual-shift practice of mixing the old with the new until the new food is in place.
✔ Monitor stool firmness and volume, coat and skin condition, and the overall appearance of your pet.
✔ If the new food passes all the tests after a month or so of trial, you may have found a new product to stay with.

Changing Foods

Don't be constantly (if ever) seeking to change foods. If your current premium food is doing all the things you want with regard to stool, hair, skin, and so forth, stay with it (consistency, remember?). Change your premium food only when conditions dictate that a change must be undertaken. Don't change because you like another food's bag color, its ads on TV, or its lowered sale price. The food your pet eats is crucial to her well-being and should not be casually changed as one might change brands of gasoline.

If you do change to a premium food and there is some hesitation on your Pom's part in continuing to eat it, give the food a chance. Feed the new food in your usual manner. If Prissy does not eat it, remove the food until the next regular feeding and give nothing else. Missing one feeding won't hurt most adult Pomeranians, and once a dog starts to eat a food, she begins to like it. Your dog will normally eat less of a premium food because it takes less of this food to meet her nutritional needs; this will also make the best premium food more economical in the long run than any cheap, bargain brand.

Food Allergies

Some dogs will develop allergic reactions to certain foods. Some Poms have problems with foods containing beef, dairy, wheat, and other grains. There are many products that use ingredients such as chicken and rice or lamb and rice and these may help avoid certain food allergies. Your veterinarian can help you recognize such allergies, isolate the cause, and find a diet that your dog's system can handle.

GROOMING YOUR POMERANIAN

The Pomeranian is not usually a difficult dog to keep well groomed, but there are certain coat considerations and some effort on the owner's part that must be taken into account. Even though the Pom is a toy breed, its ancestry is northern, doubled-coated and all!

An Overview

According to the AKC Standard, Hugo should have a coat of the following description:

"Double coated, a short, soft, thick undercoat, with longer, coarse glistening outercoat consisting of guard hairs that must be harsh to the touch in order to give the proper texture for the coat to form a frill of profuse, spreading straight hairs."

There are almost as many opinions about Pomeranian grooming as there are Pomeranian breeders, but one thing is very clear. The exacting requirements for a show dog are different than the needs of the average dog owner who has a Pom for a pet.

Grooming Show Poms

A show Pomeranian will require an excellent coat tended in a careful, consistent manner. If you are serious about pursuing a show career for your Pom, the most direct course will be the wisest. You have, of course, purchased a puppy from the best show stock available from the best available breeder. Not only will show puppy Hugo have quality coat and hair genetics but you can go to his breeder and ask questions about show grooming. If this is not possible, find the Pomeranian exhibitor whose dogs evidence the best coats and the best show preparation. Pay this person whatever (or perhaps apprentice yourself to this expert) he or she asks for lessons on how to make Hugo show-ready. Listen, learn, and follow his or her advice. But also remember, if exhibiting Hugo is your goal, then no amount of external preparation can put a good coat on him, if breeding hasn't put the potential there for a good coat.

Grooming Pet Poms

For the pet Pom owner, grooming holds no great mystery. Grooming tools for a Pomeranian consist of a good brush with natural bristles and a fine slicker brush or comb for the head, ear, and skirts. About twice a week or so, gently brush your Pomeranian to keep his coat looking good. Brush away from, or against the lay of the coat. Follow up with a fine-tooth comb on skirts and neck.

Professional Groomers

Two or three times a year or perhaps quarterly or monthly (as included in your Pomeranian budget), take Hugo to a good, professional dog groomer. Depending on your dog's special needs, a bath, a flea treatment,

═══════ TIP ═══════

Added Professional Groomer Positives

Regular visits to the groomer, who may be affiliated with a veterinarian, a quality pet products store, or a grooming shop, will also serve two other purposes. First, your Pomeranian will enjoy getting out and seeing new things. This is a good opportunity for a trip with a purpose. Second, it will be good for you to have a chance to see new dog care products, toys, or other items that may interest you. You can also take some pride in your Pomeranian and in the care you have provided. A little showing off never hurts, you or Hugo.

or both may or may not be needed. The groomer will know how to keep your Pomeranian looking good. The groomer will also attend to hair trimming in the areas of the neck, feet, anus, and anal glands, and will keep the toenails at an appropriate length.

If you find that you enjoy grooming Hugo yourself, which many pet owners do not, learn what you must do and be consistent about it. Every exhibitor should certainly know how to show-groom his or her own dog but, for a pet owner, grooming sessions are often done by a professional groomer. If you don't know a respected groomer, ask your veterinarian or pet products store to recommend one.

Using a professional groomer on a regular basis will pay off in other than grooming-

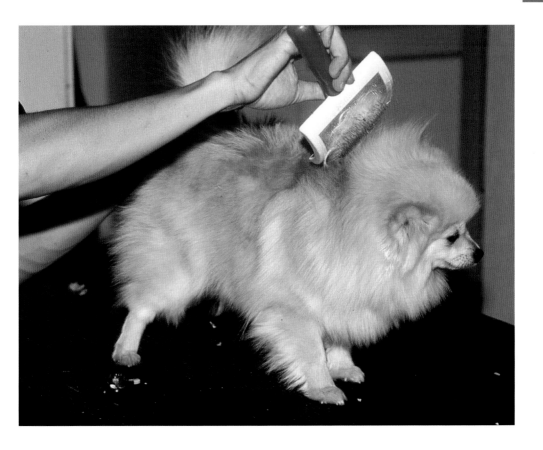

related areas: A groomer can spot parasite problems, skin conditions, and other concerns that you might miss at home. Your groomer, along with your regular veterinarian, will make up a team that will keep things pleasant and healthy for Hugo's teeth, ears, eyes, and nails. A good groomer can be a great aid to you in caring for your Pomeranian. Take time to find the best possible groomer, and encourage an active interest in your Pom. Take the groomer's advice as that of a professional who wants the best for your pet.

Start Early

As with most other aspects of the Pomeranian, an early introduction to brushing and grooming is best for the Pom puppy so that Hugo will not fear or dislike these activities. Begin as early as possible to help your puppy learn that daily brushing can be a pleasant interlude for both of you.

As a young puppy, take Hugo to your chosen groomer and introduce him not only to the groomer but to the sights, sounds, and smells of the place. Groomers will often take time to

place a clipper next to the puppy and let it feel the warmth and vibration while being gently held. This works wonders in helping to avoid fear later on.

Ask Hugo's groomer to show you how to keep your Pom's ears clean and healthy. You will want to ask this same question of Hugo's veterinarian about your dog's teeth and gums.

Pom Coat Phases

It is important to know that all Poms go through phases when their coats are not at their best. The fluffy puppy you bought from a respected breeder at eight weeks of age will usually begin to radically shed its coat when it is about four months old and the coat will look really ragged.

The adult coat will begin to show up at about six months of age, as will evidence of the puppy's final adult color. The adult coat may hold on up to about a year, when normally your Pom will shed his coat and look ragged again. This is especially true of male Poms. Females tend to shed in conjunction with their coming into season, which is just another reason for spaying.

Regular weekly brushing will keep these shedding periods easier to manage. A puppy that has been taught to enjoy the regular brushing sessions will not be difficult to handle when shedding makes brushing all the more important and all the more essential.

There are also dry bath powders (available at the veterinarian's or at the pet products store) that can help you avoid the full water bath that can dry out Hugo's skin if done too often. The dry bath can be dusted in and then combed and brushed out with no dry skin reaction. If you do want to give him a full water bath, always use a mild shampoo formulated especially for DOGS. Be sure to rinse thoroughly, getting all the soap out of Hugo's hair. Then re-rinse just to be doubly sure, and gently use a blow dryer to bring back Hugo's good looks.

With the regular care of a good professional groomer, your frequent brushing, and your touch-up cleaning a couple of times a week, your Pomeranian will stay in presentable shape. You will always want Hugo to look his best.

TIP

Partial Bath

A useful technique that many Pomeranian owners use is the partial bath that can be given a couple of times a week: Using a warm, damp washcloth, wash Hugo's underside and make sure that no fecal material has adhered to the hair around the anus. This is especially useful in keeping the urine smell off the penis and surrounding area of your male Pomeranian.

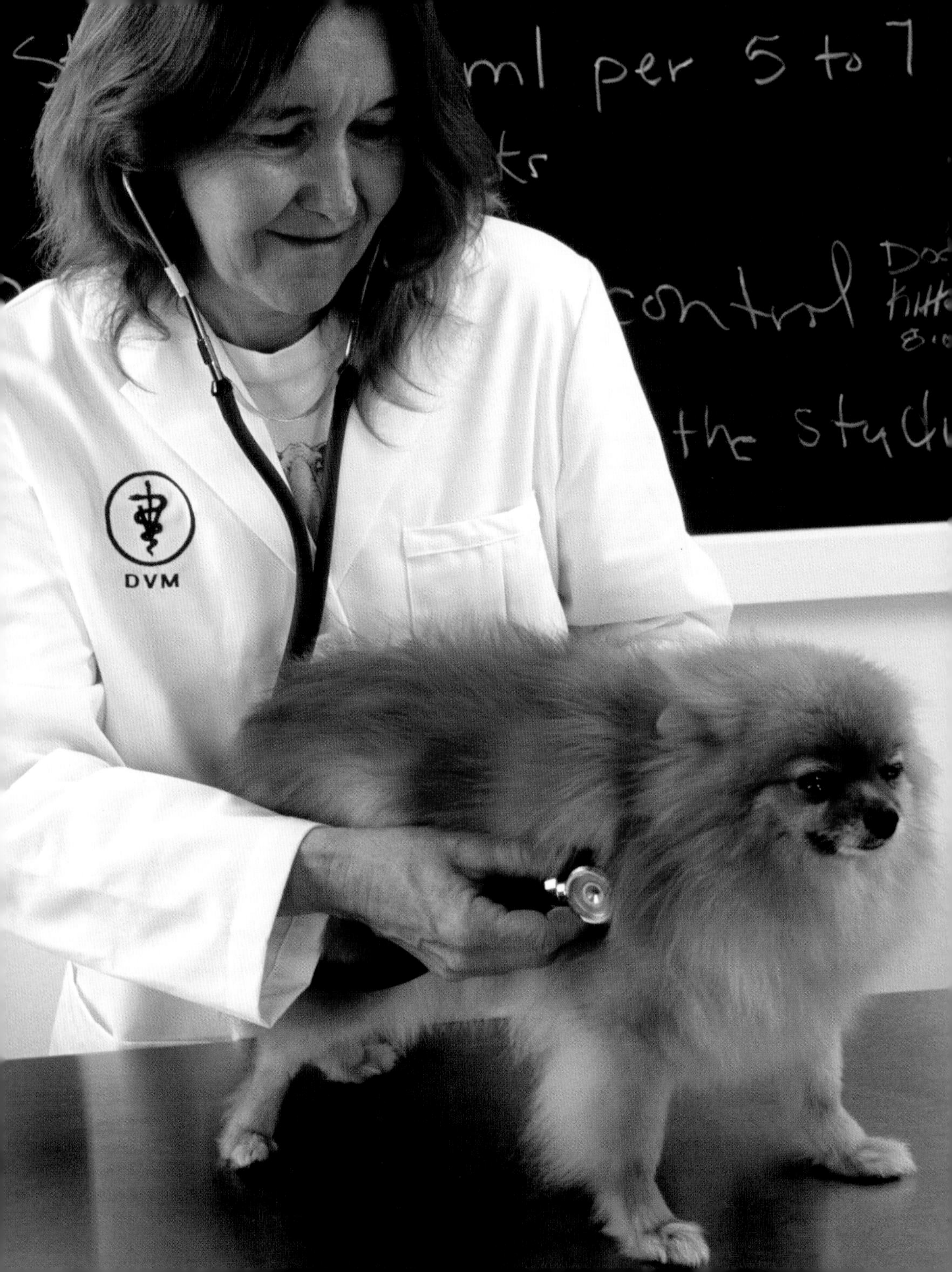
ml per 5 to 7
control
DVM

MEDICAL CARE

Preventing health problems is far less costly, and far less painful, than treating health problems. By creating a healthy environment and by having a preventive orientation, you can accomplish much in the way of keeping Prissy safe from injuries, diseases, and other unhealthy conditions.

Maintaining Health

You already know about the possible health hazards posed by small children and big dogs. You already know about puppy-proofing your home. You already know about the potential bone breaking that can come from even moderate jumping, falls, or misdirected human feet. Now here is some additional information you can add to your stock of knowledge. Armed with the ways to stop problems before they occur, you are on your way to keeping Prissy as healthy as possible for as long at she lives.

You and your family have already learned some accident-prevention ideas. Now you need to learn about the most common diseases, parasites, and medical conditions that may confront Prissy and how to recognize these health enemies.

As mentioned, Prissy's groomer is in an excellent position to monitor several aspects of your dog's health. Not only does a skilled,

professional groomer bring a good deal of expertise and experience to your team, he or she also sees your dog often enough to know a lot about her and rarely enough to notice any subtle changes that may be too gradual to be easily spotted by you and your family, who see Prissy every day. Make it a point to let the groomer know that his or her opinion is respected and welcome in matters concerning the health of your Pom.

The Veterinarian

The key member of this health team is, of course, your veterinarian. Nobody is better trained or more knowledgeable about how to keep your Pomeranian healthy than her veterinarian. The best use of a veterinarian is not only in an emergency, but as a caring professional who sees your pet on regular visits. Take time to establish a good rapport with this key team member. The veterinarian's skill and knowledge will be vital from Prissy's puppyhood to her old age.

Strive for good, clear communication with your Pom's veterinarian. He or she will need to know accurate information, without embellishment, to make the proper diagnosis and prescribe an effective treatment. Ask questions and make sure you understand the answers. Neither you nor the veterinarian can really help your Pomeranian with partial or inaccurate knowledge.

Find a good veterinarian and then follow his or her instructions—*carefully and in every way!*

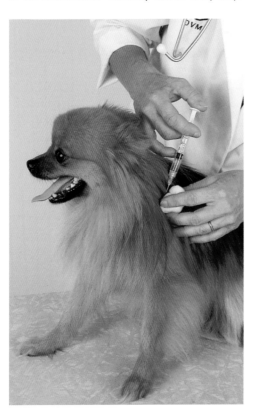

You may have a great deal of knowledge about a great many things, but trust the medical care of your pet to the person with the best training—your veterinarian.

Preventive Care

Your in-home health care and routine visits to the veterinarian provide the basis for continuing good health for your Pomeranian, but the best veterinarian in the world can't help Prissy if you don't take her to the veterinarian's office on a regular schedule.

This schedule will include visits for checkups and for vaccinations. Checkups will spot many potential health problems before they arise; vaccinations will protect your Pomeranian from a number of diseases and infections. Having your Pom immunized against a number of diseases isn't just smart; in some places, it's the law.

Vaccinations

Prissy should have received her first immunizations while still under the breeder's care.

Guideline Schedule for Core Vaccines for Pomeranian Puppies*

Vaccine	First Inoculation	Second Inoculation	Third Inoculation	First Booster	Follow-up
	Age	Age	Age	Interval	Interval
Distemper	8 weeks	12 weeks	16 weeks	1 year	Every 3 years
Canine adenovirus-2 Hepatitis	8 weeks	12 weeks	16 weeks	1 year	Every 3 years
Parvovirus**	8 weeks	12 weeks	16 weeks	1 year	Every 3 years
Rabies***	12 weeks to 16 weeks (state laws vary)			1 year	Every 3 years

*Vaccination Schedule provided by Sharon L. Vanderlip, DVM, author of *The Pomeranian Handbook,* copyright © 2007 by Barron's Educational Series, Inc.
**Some veterinarians recommend a fourth parvovirus vaccination at 20 weeks of age because many dogs do not develop sufficient immunity against this disease before they are five months of age.
***Check with your veterinarian for the timing of the rabies vaccination. It is not recommended to be given at the same time as DHPP vaccine.

The first shots include initial vaccinations for Canine distemper (Modified Live Virus vaccine or MLV), Canine parvovirus (MLV), Canine adenovirus-2/hepatitis (MLV), leptospirosis (optional), parainfluenza (optional), and *bordetella* (optional). At eight weeks of age, she should have gotten the vaccinations that her veterinarian recommended. Follow-up shots will be necessary for most of these immunizations and your veterinarian will set up a schedule. They are usually needed at 12 weeks and again at 16 weeks. These diseases, plus rabies, an immunization for which is given at 12 to 16 weeks (depending on the laws in your state), require booster shots at one year and then every three years for follow-up shots.

Some of the Diseases Controlled by Vaccinations

Be sure your veterinarian has a complete record of all vaccinations and other treatments Prissy received before you got her. This is the beginning of your Pom's health record, which should be kept up to date as long as she lives.

Canine Distemper (CD): Once the most deadly killer of puppies and young dogs, distemper is a disease that is both widespread and highly contagious. Distemper affects all the members of the canine family and a number of other small mammals. It was not uncommon, a number of years ago, for distemper to rage through a kennel and destroy most of the young dogs and all of the puppies.

As a viral disease, the onset of symptoms would rapidly appear about a week after exposure to an infected animal. At first, distemper would resemble a cold with a fever and a runny nose. The dog would then typically stop eating and appear tired and listless. Sometimes, vomiting or diarrhea would be present and the skin leathers of the nose and pads of the feet would thicken, which prompted old time dog breeders to label distemper as "hard pad disease."

Although some dogs would seem to recover, distemper would linger and later reappear in the form of convulsions, nervous twitching, paralysis, and eventually, death. Thankfully, vaccination has greatly decreased the incidence of this dreadful disease.

Rabies: As Prissy grows up, she will need a rabies vaccination. She will also require peri- odic rabies booster shots throughout her life. Rabies or *hydrophobia* was the feared "mad dog" disease that occurred periodically since earliest time among dogs and other animals. The mere mention of the word can still conjure up terrible mental pictures of mad dogs, foaming at the mouth and running amok terrorizing a neighborhood.

Rabies is an acute infectious disease of warm-blooded mammals, including man, transmitted most commonly by a bite. Skunks, raccoons, bats, and foxes are among the wild animals thought to be the most common carriers of rabies. Rabies still affects populations of wild animals in some parts of the world (including many places in the United States), but has been effectively eradicated in England and other countries largely by the use of strict quarantines.

Because of the fatal nature of the disease, its frightening symptoms, and the relative ease of transmission in earlier times, rabies joined the bubonic plague, leprosy, anthrax, and a few other so-called *nightmare* diseases that have been largely eradicated, thanks to advances in medicine. Louis Pasteur in 1885 developed the first vaccine against rabies. His early work, crude by modern standards, set the stage for a number of other immunizations that have made rabies a rare disease among humans— about one case a year occurs in the United States—but a disease that every dog should be vaccinated against!

Leptospirosis: Leptospirosis (a disease against which your veterinarian may or may not recommend immunizing in the case of house dogs, including Pomeranians) is another canine disease that can be transmitted to humans. This bacterial disease is most commonly spread by exposure to an animal with leptospirosis or by ingestion of water that has been polluted by the urine of an infected animal.

When out on walks or on trips to the dog park, keep Prissy away from puddles and standing water that may have been polluted by a sick canine. Many smart pet owners carry bottles of fresh water and a small bowl with them to avoid just such a problem.

You can recognize leptospirosis by a loss of appetite, fever, vomiting, and diarrhea. In advanced cases, serious damage to the liver and kidneys can result. Jaundice, weak hindquarters, sores in the soft tissue in the mouth, and abdominal pain are also symptoms that dogs infected with leptospirosis might evidence.

Canine Parvovirus: Parvovirus attacks the intestines of dogs. It causes a viral infection than can result in death for many unvacci-

nated or untreated dogs at any time, but especially affects puppies less than four months of age.

Listlessness and loss of appetite, followed by vomiting, as well as heavy, sometimes bloody diarrhea, are classic parvovirus symptoms. Infected puppies will suffer from extreme dehydration. Unless the dog receives prompt veterinary care, death will often be the outcome. If medical care is given to offset the effects of the dehydration and to handle any secondary infections, there is a reasonable chance of survival.

Parvovirus can be controlled by vaccination and common sense. Any unvaccinated dog should be viewed as a potential carrier. If Prissy is not vaccinated and should encounter a dog infected with parvovirus on the street during your walks, you could be inviting this dangerous virus to attack her.

To avoid exposure to many diseases, very young Pomeranian puppies should be carried when in locations where many other dogs have walked. This includes parks, pet products stores, the veterinarian's walkway and waiting room.

Hepatitis: Now known as CAV-1 (Canine Adenovirus 2), infectious canine hepatitis can affect a dog of any age. The severity of the disease can range from a relatively light ailment to a death-dealing viral infection that can cause some dogs to die in less than a day after the symptoms first appear.

The symptoms of this disease are listlessness, fever, tonsillitis, abdominal pain, vomiting, and hemorrhaging.

Parainfluenza: (Immunization may be optional, according to Prissy's veterinarian's recommendation.) Commonly called "kennel cough," parainfluenza is a highly contagious

viral disease. It can spread quickly through dogs that are kept near one another, as in a kennel, but is certainly not limited to kennels. Parainfluenza brings on tracheobronchitis, which is characterized by a dry, hacking cough followed by retching to expel throat mucus.

Parainfluenza, in and of itself, is not usually that debilitating. Untreated, however, this so-called "kennel cough" can leave a dog very susceptible to more severe respiratory ailments and secondary infections. As with the other preventable diseases, parainfluenza can be prevented by vaccination. Good treatment for tracheobronchitis is best provided by a veterinarian with the canine patient kept away from other dogs to lessen the contagion.

Prissy's veterinarian will help you keep track of the immunizations that she has had. It is *your* job, however, to see that Prissy has regularly scheduled clinical visits to help her stay safe and healthy.

Parasites

Internal Parasites

Prissy is a very small dog and thus cannot withstand large infestations of internal parasites that some larger dogs can.

Worms are common in adult dogs and puppies, and can pose serious health problems. Your veterinarian can find out if worms are present in your Pomeranian and will prescribe the most appropriate treatment. Remember that worms in a pet can also sometimes affect a pet owner.

Worms are generally detected by microscopic examination of fecal material. (Heartworms are discovered through a blood test.) The most common worms infecting dogs are roundworms, hookworms, tapeworms, heartworms, and whipworms. Each of these must be dealt with by a specific treatment from your veterinarian.

Roundworms: Roundworms are most often found in puppies, although dogs of any age can be infested. Puppies generally get roundworms even before they are born if the mother dog has them.

Puppies that have roundworms will not thrive. Their appearance is often just not quite as sharp and shiny as uninfected puppies. They may have a pendulous abdomen (potbelly). They may also pass worms through their stool or when they vomit. Your veterinarian can handle the medical aspects of eliminating roundworms after making a stool examination first and an evaluation of the dog later.

Good housekeeping on your part will help eliminate these parasites. Keep the puppies' area extremely clean and sanitized, and safely dispose of any and all stools promptly.

Hookworms: Although hookworms will infect dogs of all ages, these bloodsuckers will really cause your puppies to do poorly. The puppies have bloody or inky stools, fail to maintain weight, and fail to eat properly. Since hookworms attach themselves to the small intestine and suck blood, anemia can be the sometimes fatal result.

See your veterinarian promptly and keep Prissy away from infested areas. As with roundworms, dispose of all stools as soon as possible.

Tapeworms: Tapeworms are commonly transmitted by fleas. Although they rarely debilitate a dog these flat, segmented parasites can rob Prissy of her health.

Your veterinarian can treat Prissy and assist you in a plan to prevent the tapeworm's return. This parasite is just another good reason for eliminating fleas from your dog's environment (see discussion of fleas that follows).

Heartworms: This wide-ranging worm is transmitted to dogs by a mosquito. The mosquito, itself infested with the heartworm larvae, passes these larvae into a dog's bloodstream through bites to the dog's body tissue and ultimately to her heart.

Just because Prissy is predominantly an inside dog, don't ignore the preventive treatment that can keep this deadly and serious parasite from clogging your dog's heart. Your veterinarian can help you with medications that will prevent infestation. These medications, carefully administered, will prevent the need for an expensive, possibly risky, and prolonged treatment and save your pet from an early and miserable death.

Whipworms: Whipworms, so named because of their threadlike appearance, attach themselves to the walls of a dog's large intestine. Here they feed and lay their eggs, which are spread through the feces; another animal comes along and eats the whipworm eggs, and the whole cycle starts over again.

In mild cases, whipworms can be hard to detect. In severe instances, as the worms grow, dogs become anemic, lose weight, and are plagued by diarrhea. Heavy infestations in a dog's yard or kennel area require an increase in visits to the veterinarian.

External Parasites

Fleas: Fleas are the bane of many a dog's existence. They are the most common external parasite afflicting dogs. They feed on your

---

TIP

Flee Fleas!

Fleas are among the worst enemies you and your Pomeranian can have. Not only do they bring problems such as tapeworms and fleabite allergy, but they turn a happy Pom's life into one of constant turmoil—biting and scratching, scratching and biting. Deal with fleas in the strongest terms possible, for you and your Pomeranian!

dog's blood and in extreme cases cause anemia. Generally, they can make your Pomeranian miserable, and, since many Poms live inside, fleas can make dog owners miserable too. Your dog can even become infected with a kind of tapeworm transmitted by fleas.

Some Pomeranians suffer from flea bite allergy. While fleas are bothersome to all dogs, dogs that are allergic to fleas suffer much more. Hair loss, skin problems, and incessant scratching may indicate this allergy. Prompt treatment by a veterinarian can do much to alleviate this uncomfortable condition.

Flea bite allergy is also another good reason for working diligently to eliminate fleas from Prissy's environment and to keep them out. Dealing with fleas involves a warfare mentality—a *them-or-us* kind of thinking. You have to hit fleas at *every* possible site in order to achieve even limited victory. Everywhere an infested dog has been will harbor fleas—the bed, the yard, the doghouse, the car, your house, your summer cottage, or anywhere you and Prissy go on a regular basis. If you fail to attack the fleas in *any* of these areas, then you have failed—*they will be back!*

Flea drops, flea shampoos, flea powder, flea collars, and flea sprays are all designed for use on the dog. Be sure to treat the Pom's "den" and her bedding. Flea foggers will provide some relief for your home. In severe cases you may need to call an exterminator. Fleas spend only about 10 percent of their time on the dog, which means that 90 percent of the time fleas are available to visit your home, yard, and so on.

There are a number of new flea-repellent products available from your veterinarian,

including new tablets that can be given orally. There are also liquid products that are applied topically on the dog's skin once a month. New developments in flea collars have appeared that keep fleas off Prissy rather than killing the fleas once they arrive. Some of these new products kill flea eggs; others target only adult fleas. Your veterinarian can advise you about these new flea fighters.

Regular monthly grooming by a professional will spot fleas before they get to the severe stage. But always remember, you cannot beat a flea infestation by dealing with just part of the problem. The *entire* environment must be treated!

Ticks: On walks or while playing outside, your Pomeranian can come in contact with another vicious bloodsucker, the tick. Although regular medications will control ticks rather well, you need to know how to handle them if you see them.

Ticks are much larger than fleas, and as they engorge on blood, they can get as big as a marble if left in place. Never simply pull a tick off your dog. You will leave part of its mouth in the dog, which may cause infection. To get them out cleanly:

✔ Place a drop of alcohol at the location where the tick is attached to the skin. Let the alcohol cause the tick to loosen its grip a bit.

✔ Using tweezers, grasp the tick as close to the dog's skin as possible and pull slowly. Be sure to get the mouth of the tick when you pull the pest away.

✔ Put alcohol on the bite and dispose of the tick carefully, as it can get back on the dog or on you if simply dropped on the ground.

Ticks have gained notoriety with the onset of Lyme disease in humans. This potentially life-

threatening disease is transmitted by the deer tick and has been found in many areas across the United States. If a tick bites you, save it and see a medical professional immediately to identify it!

Ear mites: One parasite that can cause Prissy great discomfort is the ear mite. These microscopic mites live in the ear canal. They cause the development of a dark waxy residue and can be easily transmitted to and from other dogs (or cats). Symptoms include head shaking and ear scratching. Prissy's veterinarian can identify and treat mites quickly and effectively.

Mange: Another problem brought to the dog by mites is mange. There are two kinds: red mange (demodectic) and scabies (sarcoptic).

Red mange especially affects old dogs and young puppies and causes scruffy hair loss and other symptoms. It varies in degree of severity from dog to dog. Itching may sometimes accompany red mange. Seek veterinary help immediately; don't mess around with mange!

Scabies mites burrow into the dog's epidermal skin layer. They are highly contagious and can spread from your dog to other dogs or to you! Sarcoptic mange causes unsightly hair loss and a lot of itching.

Your groomer may act as an early warning system here. See your veterinarian immediately for proper diagnosis and treatment.

Other skin problems: Like other dog breeds, Pomeranians are sometimes beset with any of a number of skin problems—allergies, fungi, and so on. Flea bite allergy is one skin problem that stems directly from an allergic reaction to fleas (see page 68). Some dogs may develop allergies to certain foods or to some aspect of their environment. Fuel odors, perfumes, air fresheners, cleaning solvents all may play a part in causing allergies. Prissy's veterinarian can usually pinpoint the sources of these conditions and help her by either preventing the problem or dealing with it.

One of the most unsightly problems plaguing some young adult Pomeranians is Sex Hormone Alopecia X. Alopecia X is also known as Black Skin Disease or Severe Hair Loss Syndrome (and by several other clinical names).

This condition, which may affect males more than females, could possibly be caused by a genetically sex-linked growth hormone deficiency. It is characterized by signs of hair loss from the Pom's backside, tail, neck, and both sides in a sort of symmetrical manner. Alopecia X may be hereditary, but doesn't usually show up on puppies, so you can't be on a lookout for it. This condition (treatment for which is currently being actively researched) could com-

pletely denude your handsome Pomeranian or leave large areas bare.

It is important to recognize that some other skin conditions may be of a genetic origin. Your dog's problem may be something that it inherited from its parents, just another good reason to take special care in choosing a Pomeranian puppy. Rely on your veterinarian in diagnosing and treating skin problems. Home remedies here can often make a condition much worse. Let a professional, with all the information and resources available, develop the treatment plan for Prissy. You won't regret it—nor will she!

Common Health Problems

Vomiting and Diarrhea

Some vomiting and diarrhea can result from normal factors, such as dietetic changes, or from stress, but in puppies these problems are most commonly caused by intestinal parasites and viruses. Both vomiting and diarrhea are possible indicators of other, more serious conditions. Any prolonged vomiting or diarrhea that your Pom experiences deserves at least a call to the veterinarian's office for advice. Early treatment is effective treatment. Until you have gained more experience, take care in all such situations.

If either vomiting or diarrhea becomes severe or continues for more than 12 to 24 hours, you would be wise to take your Pom to your veterinarian.

Constipation

If your Pom has not been experiencing normal bowel movements, or if she is clearly strain-

ing to defecate, constipation may be the cause. Many dietetic causes, such as eating bones or a sudden change in dog food, can cause constipation. Sometimes a Pom that has been traveling and has not been allowed relief walks on a regular basis will become constipated.

Most constipation is a minor problem, but check with your veterinarian if it continues; especially if Prissy is in obvious pain and crying out while trying to defecate.

Impacted Anal Sacs

The anal sacs lie just under the skin on each side of the anus. Normally these are emptied of their strong-smelling secretions during defeca-

tion. Sometimes, however, these sacs become clogged (impacted) and must be emptied by hand. Some groomers will provide this service. Your veterinarian can also show you how to do this. When you see Prissy scooting along the floor or ground, dragging her rear end, impacted anal sacs or possible tapeworm irritation could be the cause.

Special Health Concerns

Patellar Luxation

A luxated patella, in more common terms, is a dislocated kneecap. This condition, usually considered inherited, is common to several toy breeds, including the Pomeranian. Luxating patellas can vary with degree of severity, from cases requiring surgery to barely noticeable conditions. Veterinarians will help devise appropriate treatment modalities for each individual occurrence of this problem. Dogs with luxating patellas should not be bred regardless of the degree of severity.

Collapsing Trachea

This birth defect, often seen in toy breed dogs, causes coughing and labored breathing. As with all other health matters affecting your Pomeranian, consult with your veterinarian about this defect.

Open Fontanels

Much like young human babies, baby Pomeranians sometimes have a "soft spot" on the top of their skull. These are called open fontanels; some of the smaller open fontanels will close by the time the Pom becomes an adult. This is definitely a matter to discuss with the breeder of your puppy.

Hypothyroidism

Low thyroid affects many Pomeranians. Responsible breeders should be able to give you accurate case histories of any thyroid problems in the sire (father) and the dam (mother) of the puppy you are considering.

Anesthetic Reaction

Many toy breeds, including the Pomeranian, can have serious tolerance problems to anesthetics. Some newer anesthetics, such as Isoflurane, seem to have no contraindications for Pomeranians. Most veterinarians know about this problem of toy breeds and reactions have been greatly reduced.

Other Inherited Problems

As with many breeds, especially toy breeds, there are a number of other conditions that may be inherited; some families or strains of Poms have them more often than others. For example, Poms with extreme dwarfism, as seen in "teacup" Poms, tend to have more inherited health problems than regular Poms. Consult with Pomeranian experts about the problems observed, however rarely, in their breeding lines.

Pomeranians of some colors such as blue or other dilute colors may experience more skin trouble. The color pattern merle (see "Author's Note," page 19) can cause serious health problems if two merle patterned dogs are bred together.

Emergency Care

Hypoglycemia

Hypoglycemia or low blood sugar can be a real killer in young Pomeranians. Prissy and her Pom kin are little energy-burning machines. They can burn up any caloric reserves so it is important that these young dynamos have their nutritious, dry puppy food available to them at all times. Pomeranian puppies, and some young adults as well, simply cannot eat enough in only one daily meal to get them through their action-packed days.

Lethargy or moping, staying away from everyone with inactivity and drowsiness, may be a sign that Prissy is experiencing a drop in blood sugar. If not treated immediately she

Not So Obvious Dangers

These items can pose grave dangers in your Pom's home or in her environment (which includes walks, the park, or places you visit).

- Antifreeze—highly poisonous but has an odor and taste that attract dogs.
- De-icers and other automotive liquids.
- A number of indoor and yard plants are deadly if eaten.
- Coffee, caffeinated soft drinks, alcoholic drinks, chocolate can be toxic to most dogs.
- Some insect bites or stings can cause strong allergic reactions in your Pomeranian (bees, wasps, fire ants, ticks, fleas).
- Tobacco products (cigars and cigarettes, old quids from chewing tobacco, and nicotine patches).
- Over-the-counter and prescription drugs, vitamins and supplements, especially those with iron (Pomeranians can chew their way into almost any kind of safety cap).
- Raw potatoes, tomatoes, eggplant, rhubarb (fruits, peelings, or stems).
- Some kinds of nuts (especially macadamias) and fruit seeds (apples, pears, citrus, grapes, and raisins).
- String, yarn, thread, fishing line, extension cords, and dental floss.
- Mushrooms, toadstools, and other fungi or mold.
- Rawhide dog chews, cow and pig ears.
- Any other products that have "skull and crossbones" or ingestion warnings.
- Garbage and items left behind by careless people.
- Batteries, dry cell, and smaller specialty batteries such as those in watches, hearing aids, and car remotes.

could go into severe seizures and die. Don't wait to travel to the veterinarian. Don't try to force-feed her, which could cause Prissy to choke. Using corn syrup or a sugar-rich substance such as the product Nutri-Cal, Pedialyte, or Pet Nutri-Drops (which you can have on hand from your veterinarian or pet products store), rub this sugar source on her gums and contact her veterinarian.

To avoid hypoglycemia's often co-ailments *hypothermia* and *dehydration* (which may require some liquid electrolyte replacement product), that are part of what Sharon Vanderlip, DVM (author of *The Pomeranian Handbook*, see page 93) refers to as "The Three Deadly Dangers," cover Prissy with a blanket to keep her warm as you transport her immediately to her doctor.

Poisoning and Toxic Reactions

Protecting your Pom puppy from some toxic products and conditions has been discussed. There are other accidental poisoning possibilities you should know about that will generally require immediate veterinary care. Toxic items and products require the utmost in "protective paranoia" and common sense from every member of a Pom's family!

Be alert to listlessness, convulsions, disoriented behavior, vomiting, diarrhea, and a

If your Pomeranian has been injured, be careful not to make the injury worse or to be bitten by a dog in pain. Using a small piece of cloth, a shoestring, or a handkerchief as a muzzle, gently lift your Pom and place her on a makeshift stretcher made of your shirt, a towel, or some other cloth that will allow you to move the injured dog without danger of further injury. Call your veterinarian's office to alert the staff to the situation and safely transport your dog there.

Bleeding

If your Pomeranian appears to be bleeding, identify the source of the blood and apply firm but gentle pressure to the area. If the injury is on an extremity, control the bleeding by applying direct pressure to the wound. Continued bleeding, any significant blood loss, or a gaping wound will require immediate veterinary attention. Treat any bleeding as a very serious condition.

Heatstroke

Healthy, happy Prissy can be dying or dead in just a few minutes in a car with poor ventilation and high inside temperature. The double coat of the Pomeranian cannot insulate the dog in a closed space. Because Poms love to travel, they are often subjected to this danger, one that is frequently ignored even by caring Pomeranian owners. Just a few minutes in the sun, even on a moderately warm day—60°F (15.6°C) or so—or even with some windows partially rolled down can lead to the death of the dog.

One Pom fancier with his crated Pom, on a hot summer day, was returning from a trip to the groomer when he was stopped by the

change in the color of mucous membranes as these could signal poison ingestion or toxic interaction. Get your pet to the veterinarian as soon as possible when these symptoms appear.

Accidents

Many accidents can be prevented by just thinking ahead and being a little creatively paranoid about things that can hurt your Pom. However, as careful as you are, accidents still happen.

police for a minor traffic violation. He was asked to turn off his car, step away from the car and approach the police car to get his ticket, have his license checked, and so forth. In just that short span of time time, the Pom began to show heatstroke symptoms. Thanks to the police, now in an escort role, the dog was rushed to the veterinarian and his life was saved. *NEVER* take chances by leaving your Pom in an enclosed area unattended. It is fatal to a pet, especially a little longhaired dog.

Heatstroke symptoms include a dazed look and rapid, shallow panting with a high fever. The dog's gums will be bright red. This is one situation where you must act before going to the veterinarian. Immediately lower the dog's temperature with cool water. Rush her to the *nearest* veterinary hospital immediately.

Old Age

Aging is a natural process that will affect both you and Prissy. The bouncy puppy will give way to the young adult, which will become the mature dog, which will become your long-time companion and old friend. Pomeranians normally have a long life span, but aging is not without its adjustments. As Prissy begins to reach eight or nine years of age—some dogs age more quickly than others—certain changes will become evident. She may begin to experience certain age-related problems with her teeth and gums, joints and muscles, bowels and bladder, eyesight, and hearing. Your good preventive care that began in puppyhood, along with regular veterinarian visits, can forestall or delay many of these concerns, but if Prissy (or Hugo) live long enough, some age-related troubles will present themselves.

Euthanasia

When in the natural course of Prissy's life, age, infirmity, or terminal illness makes that life a painful, negative experience for her, you have a difficult decision to make. It is never easy to say good-bye to a loving pet whose life has made yours so much richer just by being there. It will be even harder to see that same loving pet in constant pain as she goes about even basic daily activities.

Discuss options with your veterinarian, who has taken care of Prissy for a long time and personally cares about her too. Euthanasia, although a painful decision for you, is painless and humane for your old friend. It should be considered when Prissy can no longer experience even the simply joy of existing because she is enduring a life of increasing discomfort, disability, and suffering.

Teeth

Teeth issues are fairly common in Pomeranians. Ranging from early tooth losses, misplacement of teeth, retained baby teeth, and malocclusion (teeth that fail to meet properly), Pom teeth need lots of owner and veterinary attention.

Throughout the life of your Pomeranian, tartar buildup on her teeth will be a problem. Feeding a premium-quality dry dog food will serve as an abrasive to help keep your Pom's teeth clean. Chew toys, nylon bones, and similar products will also help, but as with humans, brushing from puppyhood on will help keep down plaque and tartar.

If you use canine oral care kits, which contain a special toothbrush and *veterinary* dentifrice, on a regular basis, your Pom will have a much better chance to avoid dental problems later on. Weak, loose, missing, or decayed teeth and gum problems can plague Pomeranians and cause other health problems. You could have your veterinarian begin to clean Prissy's teeth, beginning early in her life. Her veterinarian can do full and thorough teeth cleaning, which may require general anesthesia. Remember, regular preventive care can greatly eliminate many canine dental problems.

Eyes

The Pomeranian's eyes are large and prominent. Eye care, under normal conditions, is not a major problem. Always use good preventive measures such as avoiding any sharp objects at eye level that might harm Prissy. Angry cats have already been mentioned for their danger potential (see page 24).

You may, on occasion, see some mucous-like matter collecting in the corners of her eyes. This is usually of no real consequence. Simply use a tissue and gently wipe the material out of the eyes.

As with other medical matters, use common sense. If Prissy begins to have excessive eye discharge, redness, or evident discomfort, consult immediately with her veterinarian. Pomeranians often have eye concerns and need constant inspection and current care.

Chemical Fumes

Pomeranians can suffer from exposure to chemical fumes, such as those from household cleaners, exterminating products, and so forth, or to smoke from a cigarette or a fireplace. Just a little awareness of what life is like at its level of under 12 inches (30 cm) will help you protect your Pom's eyes.

Cataracts

Older dogs, including older Pomeranians, sometimes develop cataracts, a thick opaqueness of or involving the lens. In this case, you will notice a gradual "clouding" of the eye. Cataracts can be part of the aging process. Other than the cosmetic aspects and some vision impairment, cataracts are not usually serious.

Ears

Much of the regular observation you do to guard against ear mites (see page 69) will help you monitor overall ear health. Your groomer and your veterinarian will also help you prevent problems here. If the ears begin to show inflammation or Prissy is obviously repeatedly bothered by her ears, there may be an infection. Don't delay in seeking professional care.

If your Pom has access to a wooded area, you need to know that the ears are a favorite target area for ticks. Always check for these critters if your Pom has been where ticks may be lurking (see page 69).

As with Prissy's eyes, her ears deserve daily attention. Gentle cleaning with a soft cloth or cotton ball will help alleviate any minor irritations and alert you to more serious concerns.

Nails

Part of the consistent care regimen for your Pomeranian will be regular attention to her toenails. Beginning while Prissy is still a puppy, her nails should be kept trimmed. By starting early and gently, she will not fear nail trimming, which she will need on a monthly basis for the rest of her life. Failure to keep the nails at an appropriate length can result in painful lameness for Poms, whose way of walking depends on them being up on their tiptoes.

Your groomer or Prissy's veterinarian can handle the nail trimming during a regular grooming session, but you can trim the nails yourself with a good pair of canine nail clippers and keep them neat with a good nail file. Get your groomer or veterinarian to show you how to use these especially designed canine nail clippers. Practice on round toothpicks to learn to cut off just the tip of the nail; you must avoid the "quick" or vein of the nail, which will bleed if it is cut. You can use styptic powder if you do accidentally cut the nail too short.

Administering Medicine

While much of your Prissy's health care will rest in the hands of your veterinarian, being able to administer prescription medicines is important. She may not like taking medicine and may spit out pills and capsules. One way to get pills, such as monthly heartworm medication, into the Pom is by hiding capsules and pills in some treat item, such as on a small piece of bread smeared with smooth peanut butter.

The direct approach to administering medicine is to simply open her mouth, entering from one side, tilting her head back just a little way and placing the pill as far back on her tongue as you can. Close Prissy's mouth and wait for her to swallow. *It is important not to just casually toss the pill into the dog's mouth or tilt the head back too far; the pill could be caught in the windpipe instead of going down the throat.* Liquid medicine is administered in a similar way by tilting her head back only slightly and pouring the liquid dosage into the back of her mouth.

TRAINING YOUR POMERANIAN

Hugo, your cute, cuddly Pomeranian puppy, is a pack animal just like the wolf, the sled dog, or the foxhound. Pack behavior is a natural, integral part of your puppy and exists as the key to teaching him to be a well-trained, good canine citizen.

Pack Behavior

The pack, in simple terms, is a canine caste system where each member has and knows his place. The pack provides security and a sense of belonging that is crucial to a well-adjusted dog. Positioning in the pack hierarchy is usually based on physical strength and experience. Within it the strongest and most savvy male fills the role of "alpha" or first male.

The alpha dog leads the pack. He adjudicates differences between pack members, enforces his will on the pack, and helps train the young or inexperienced in what is expected of them as pack members. He remains the alpha dog as long as he is the strongest. You will have to perform this role for Hugo, and your family will have to serve as the pack members. Your puppy will have already been taught pack

behavior by his mother and littermates. You and the other members of your household will be a logical and necessary extension of what the mother dog began.

Training will be much more easily accomplished if you follow the example of Hugo's mother. She taught him, almost from the moment of his birth, lessons he would need to survive. As he grew, she reprimanded him, loved him, and instructed him in a pattern that you can and should follow:

1. She admonished Hugo *quickly* for any misdeeds, while the puppy, with his short attention span, could identify action with outcome.

2. She corrected Hugo *fairly*, neither overreacting nor underreacting to his misdeed.

3. She was *consistent* in her treatment of the puppy. A particular behavior did not get

═══ **TIP** ═══

Don't Let Your Pom Get the Upper Paw!

Pomeranians are bright and independent dogs. If you seem weak and indecisive at any point in caring for your Pomeranian, you may create a headstrong little entity unto himself. If Hugo gets the idea that you can be bullied out of something, rest assured he will remember that and test the boundaries. Be stronger than your Pom! Don't let the little seven-pound dog assume that he is the boss and you work for him!

Hugo a loving lick one time and a warning growl the next.

4. She went about her training *without anger.* She didn't savagely attack Hugo for a misdeed, nor did she bark at him endlessly in an effort to "verbalize" the puppy into correct behavior.

5. She showed Hugo that she *loved* him and made him feel secure, even if he had done something that had warranted correction earlier in the day. She didn't withhold love to force the puppy to act correctly.

There is much to learn from the lessons taught by the mother dog. Not only does Hugo already understand these lessons, but the lessons worked for his mother and will work for you!

When you take Hugo away from his mother and the security of the pack, you should immediately move to fill this gap. You and your family would do well to understand the role of the pack in Hugo's emotional well-being. You, or your designated person, must become the alpha dog to help this youngster learn his lessons. Hugo will want to please you after he knows that you love him and will care for him. How your Pom goes about learning what he must do to please you is up to you. Hugo won't learn these lessons by simple osmosis; he must be trained.

When to Begin

Some lessons, such as house-training and basic rules, can begin immediately. More involved training should begin between five and eight months, based on Hugo's own time-table. Some Pomeranian puppies are ready earlier than others. Don't push Hugo to be an

"early bloomer." Let him learn what he can in the security of the home, and when he seems ready—physically and mentally mature—for further training, move on to the next step.

Training Essentials

✔ You and Hugo will need a regularly set time—perhaps a couple of times a day—free from distractions such as other dogs, running children, and so forth. This time should be short, not more than 15 minutes, and while enjoyable, it should be work time not playtime.

✔ You need to have a clear idea—perhaps discussed with other members of your family—of what you want Hugo to learn. Consistency is important. You can't be correcting behavior that everyone else in the family ignores or even rewards.

✔ You are the boss, the alpha dog. Use a stern tone of voice during the training sessions to differentiate from other times when you and the Pom are together. This is an authoritarian hat, but not a drill sergeant's hat. These sessions should never be conducted when you are angry at Hugo, your spouse, your boss, or the government.

✔ Each session should be conducted as a class. Learning is the objective. If the command *"Come"* is to be taught today, don't try to get into the variations of *"Fetch"* or *"Roll over."* Stay on the subject. Review previous lessons and praise Hugo when he does something right. Correct *each* time he doesn't do what he should, but make sure that Hugo understands the desired action. If you can't get a lesson across, go back to something he does do well. Repeat that correct command several times,

then praise Hugo and end the session. Always end on a positive!

✔ Use appropriate praise for a successfully learned behavior. This doesn't mean Hugo does what you want one time and then you spend the rest of the time playing. Praise effectively, but save play for later, allowing a few minutes of lag time between the lesson and playtime so that the two are not confused.

✔ Correct misdeeds immediately while you can so that the puppy can identify the action or misdeed with your reprimand. Don't attempt to punish Hugo for something he has done some time ago. He won't remember or understand why you are reprimanding him; free-floating reprimands don't do anything but confuse him when what you want to do is change his behavior.

✔ Be patient and never lose your temper. Ranting and raving or whipping him (verbally or physically) can ruin Hugo's trust in you. Remember the lack of anger the mother dog used with the puppies.

Discipline

As mentioned previously, Hugo should *never* be the victim of physical punishment. If you follow the previous training-session design, a stern voice using the word *"No"* in a firm manner will convey your displeasure.

Some dogs, especially some independently minded Pomeranians, will test the limits of your control and your ability to be the alpha dog. Just because Hugo is small doesn't mean this testing won't take place. Counter any such behavior immediately and consistently. You are the alpha dog and as such you can't allow such behavior.

Setting the Stage

Hugo will need to learn his name early in your relationship. If your dog is a registered Pom from a long line of champions, he may have an impressive or even pretentious formal name. It is amazing how a tiny puppy that just fits in your hand could have a moniker such as "Marcy's Luscious Lothar of Barr Sinister." He will need a short name that will be his

━━━━━━ TIP ━━━━━━

Rewards, Treats, or Praise

Different dog trainers use different reward systems to reinforce training. My personal bias has always been to rely primarily on praise. That is not to say that treats (generally tasty, quickly downed bits of liver or other delights) can't be extremely effective. It is good to remember that you are dealing with a strong-willed little dog in the Pomeranian that may or may not get the idea that the only reason to obey a command is to get a taste treat.

You can use treat rewards to help get training started if praise doesn't work, but remember you may not always have treats with you and you will still want obedience.

"call name," preferably of one or two syllables. Name your puppy and stick with that name. Have your family stick with it. If the dog's call name is Hugo, call him Hugo, not the *Hugo-meister* or *Hugey Poo*. Your Pomeranian definitely needs to know what his name is in order for training to begin.

Basic Training

When Hugo is about five months old, you can be reasonably sure that he is mature enough to learn the basic obedience commands that will make him a more manageable pet. Unfortunately, some owners of toy breeds fail to give their pets the advantages of training. They seem to feel that their little dog can be carried and therefore be made to do what

is required. These people and their pets are missing one of the great joys of human-canine interaction—the ability of the human to find a way to communicate with the canine and shape the canine's behavior, having a good time in the process.

Collar and Leash

A web or nylon training collar is the most effective and humane way to train Hugo. When you use the collar correctly, the collar does not choke the dog; it merely provides

restraining, correcting pressure when given a slight tug upward. This gets Hugo's attention and also serves as a correcting method. The gentle tug and the stern word *"No"* let the puppy know he has done wrong. The collar will need to be large enough to go over your Hugo's head at its widest part with about one inch to spare but not much more. This collar is generally used for training only. Before beginning the lesson, exchange your Pom's regular collar, the one attached to his personal identification and rabies vaccination tags, for the training collar.

With the training collar you will need a 1/2- to 1-inch (1.3–2.5 cm) wide leash (or lead) measuring about 6 feet (1.8 m) long. The lead can be leather, web, or nylon. It will need to have a swivel snap at one end for fastening through the ring on the training collar. At the other end, the lead should have a comfortable hand loop. This lead is, of course, longer than your normal walking leash.

You should familiarize Hugo with the training collar and with the lead in a carefully orches- trated way so that he will not come to fear or dislike either the collar or the lead. In a large room where there are no obstacles to snag the lead and frighten the puppy, let your Pom run around with the training collar on and the lead trailing along behind. This will give him the feel of the weight of the collar and lead before training time actually rolls around.

Basic Commands

There are five basic commands: *sit, down, stay, heel,* and *come.* With these five skills firmly in his repertoire, Hugo will be a better pet or you both could even pursue further training in the Obedience ring if he has the aptitude and you are so inclined. Be sure to issue clear, one-word commands to your dog, such as *"Sit."* Use the dog's name before each command and be authoritarian in your tone: *"Hugo, sit!"* Use the same tone each time. Don't confuse him by using two commands at one time, such as *"Sit down."* Also remember

the keys to canine learning are wrapped up in four rules:

1. Praise enthusiastically.
2. Correct fairly and immediately.
3. Practice consistent repetition.
4. Don't lose your temper.

Sit

The *sit* is a good command. Hugo already knows how to sit; all you need to do is teach him when and where to do it.

✔ With the training collar on and attached to the lead, place Hugo on your left side next to your left leg, while holding the lead in your right hand.

✔ In one continuous, gentle motion, pull his head up with the lead as you push his hind-quarters gently down with your left hand, giving a firm command, *"Sit,"* as you do so.

✔ When Hugo is in the sitting position, lavishly praise him.

Using the concept of consistent repetition, repeat the lesson, until he sits down without his rear end being pushed. Remember to keep the same gentle upward pressure on the lead to prevent a *sit* from becoming a belly flop. If Hugo shifts in position, use your left hand to move him back to where he belongs. Keep doing this exercise until he associates the word *"Sit"* and your tone with the praise he gets if he sits down. Soon Hugo will sit upon hearing the word alone without the rear-end push or the raised lead. Always use praise liberally. Make the praise and the lesson stick out in Hugo's mind.

Keep your training time brief. Initially, don't leave him in the sitting position long enough to bore him. Gradually increase the time for sitting. Remember, consistent repetition with

praise and correction will help Hugo learn. You may have to begin again at each training time for a while. He will learn more quickly with several brief, consistent sessions than with one long, drawn-out session.

Stay

Do not attempt to teach *stay* until Hugo is doing well with *sit*. The *stay* begins from the *sit* and without that foundation, the *stay* command cannot be mastered.

✔ To begin your part of the *stay* command, you must place Hugo in a regular sitting position on your left. Keep some gentle pressure on the lead in your right hand to keep the Pom's head up.

✔ Giving the clear, authoritative command *"Stay!"* step straight (forward) away from the dog, moving your right foot first. At the same time, bring the palm of your left hand down in front of Hugo's face. Your command, the stepping away, moving the right foot first, and the hand signal must be simultaneous and done exactly the same way in each repetition.

✔ Keep eye contact with him and repeat the *stay* command in the same firm tone as before.

Don't really expect long *stays* initially. Praise Hugo for his *stays* whatever their length, but if he moves toward you, take him back to the starting point, make him sit, and start again with consistent repetition. Patience is the rule here. Hugo loves you and wants to come and be with you. If he has trouble with the *stay*, don't wear him down trying; go back to the *sit*, a command that he can do well, and enthusiastically praise him, always ending difficult lessons with something easy and with lavish reward.

Each time Hugo obeys the *stay* command, praise him. You will be able to gradually move further away and he will eventually get the idea. Introduce the release word *"Okay"* in a cheerful, happy way when you want to let him know that he can now come to you and be appropriately rewarded with praise.

Because of the conflicts the puppy feels—wanting to please you and wanting to be with you—the *stay* is fairly difficult, but with patience and consistency you will see Hugo master it.

Heel

Now that the training collar and lead are part of your dog's experience, you can teach him to *heel*, a most useful and necessary thing to learn.

✔ Begin *heel* training with Hugo on your left side, his head next to your left foot, in the *sit* position.

✔ Holding the lead in your right hand and leading with your left foot, step forward saying in your firm, authoritative "alpha" voice, *"Heel!"* Use the dog's name to begin the command as in, *"Hugo, heel!"*

✔ If he doesn't move out when you do, snap the lead sharply against your leg and repeat the command, walking away as you do. As soon as Hugo catches up with you, praise him but keep moving, using encouraging praise as long as he stays with you in proper position.

✔ When you stop, tell Hugo *"Sit!"* As he becomes more experienced (through consistent and patient repetition) in heeling, he will learn to sit on his own when you stop. Don't let Hugo lag behind or run ahead or edge around to face you. The purpose of the *heel* command is not just to walk your dog but to position him on your left and teach him to move and stop when you move and stop. The ultimate goal of heeling would be to have Hugo accomplish this without the necessity of the lead.

Don't drag Hugo along behind you just to cover some distance. Always go back to the *sit* and start again. The *heel* command is difficult for some dogs to learn. Continue your use of gentle tugs on the lead to keep Hugo moving and keep his head in line with your left leg. Like most Pomeranians he is intelligent and can pick up heeling in consistent, patient lessons.

Down

Down begins with the *sit* and the *stay*.

✔ Using the lead in an *opposite* movement from the upward pressure used with the *sit* and the *stay*, pull down on the lead with your right hand, presenting the palm of your left hand with a downward motion in front of Hugo's face while clearly giving the command

"*Down!*" The small size of the Pom makes this easy to do.

✔ If the dog doesn't want to go downward, put the lead under your left foot and pull up on it, gently forcing the Pom's head downward. Again use the hand signal and the command, "*Down!*"

✔ Once Hugo is in the *down* position, heap on the praise. You can help your puppy just a bit in the early lessons for this command by using your left hand, as in the *sit* command, but gently push on the back rather than on the hindquarters. It is the downward direction that this command strives to emphasize, but it should be used in conjunction with the *stay*. The ultimate goal is to cause Hugo to go straight down on his stomach and remain there until released by the "*Okay*" command from you.

The *down* can be a very useful and important command to stop your Pom in his tracks when he might be heading for trouble or danger. Practice the *down* together with *sit* and *stay;* always make sure that Hugo is rewarded when he stays in the *down* position. Using the credo of consistent repetition, you should be able to gradually increase the length of the *down* and even leave his line of sight and expect him to remain in place. As with the *stay,* Hugo should not move about. Correct him if he does; praise him if he doesn't.

Come

The *come* command may seem simple, but there are several important elements to it. With the lead (or even a longer leash attached for this lesson) and collar attached, the *come* command can begin. Enthusiasm and use of his name and the command with wide open arms will let Hugo know you really want to be with him. This seems like a natural behavior, yet so many unthinking people foolishly call their dogs to them and then scold, punish, or even whip them. To an intelligent Pomeranian puppy, the command "*Come*" issued by you, or any member of your family, then followed by a reprimand, could cause this naturally happy behavior to be unlearned quickly. *Never* call your dog to you and correct or discipline him. If the dog must be corrected, you go to the dog and do it.

✔ Always heap loads of praise on Hugo when he comes at your call. Remember that he must learn that *come,* like the other commands, must be obeyed immediately *each and every time.*

✔ If Hugo is a little stubborn or inattentive to the command; give the lead, which of course is still in use, a firm but gentle tug to get movement in your direction started. This method will work, especially when combined with the authoritative command from you as the alpha leader and the warm tones and friendly gesturing that follow it. If not, you can use a little firmer tug with the command.

✔ As in other lessons and other commands, have Hugo on a 6-foot (2-m) lead, but a longer lead can be used—up to 20 feet (6 m)—to reinforce the *come* command from a greater distance.

One point in the *come* command differs from the others. This command does *not* need to be repeated over and over again during a lesson. Use it when you are working on the other lessons or when your dog is involved in play or something else. Always expect the dog to obey this command quickly and praise the dog when he complies.

Remember that saying *"Come"* and then reprimanding is an excellent way to untrain Hugo. Teach this important point to your family. While discussing this with your family, let each person learn all the different commands and the correct "hows" and "whys" of each part. This will make things much saner for Hugo, because he can't possibly learn when he is getting conflicting usages of the same words from different members of his "pack."

Obedience Classes

If, for whatever reason, you can't seem to teach your Pomeranian, don't hesitate to enlist the help of a professionally run obedience school or dog training class. Another option is a local dog club where obedience lessons

are frequently offered. Recognize that much of what will be taught in these classes will be aimed at helping you train yourself to train your dog. There are many other things that your bright Hugo can learn beyond the basic commands discussed here. You may want to give your puppy or adult dog a chance at higher education.

Obedience Trials

Obedience trials have become one of the fastest-growing dog-related activities in the United States. If you and Hugo are suited for this activity, you may want to see what obedience trials are all about.

You can get a copy of the rules from the AKC. This will give you all you need to know about Novice Class competitions. Obedience work isn't for every dog owner or for every dog, but for those who want to learn the various titles (CD, Companion Dog; CDX, Companion Dog Excellent; UD, Utility Dog; OT Ch, Obedience Trial Champion) it can be a wonderful undertaking.

The United Kennel Club (UKC) and the Canadian Kennel Club (CKC) also sanction very similar obedience trials. Pomeranians are eligible for these trials also.

Barking Behavior

As mentioned earlier, Pomeranians are alert, vocal little dogs that show an interest in everything and everyone. When this interest takes the form of unwarranted barking, some training techniques need to be applied to the problem. Again, the prevention is much better than the cure.

Beginning with the very young puppy on his first night with you, if you let his sad crying cause you to pick him up repeatedly, then you are training that puppy to do something that later you will not like.

Just as you should never encourage begging behavior by feeding tidbits at the dinner table, you can keep yourself from teaching unwarranted barking in much the same way. Simply don't respond to barking when you don't want barking to occur. If Hugo is barking just to get your attention, steel yourself—and teach this to your family—and ignore him. Pay attention to him only when there has been no unwarranted barking. It takes time, but if you are patient and consistent, it works.

While housetraining isn't that hard for many Pomeranians, there are some definite ways to make this key training easier for your pet. Follow these hints to help ease Hugo along the path that leads to housetraining:

1. Take Hugo to the "relief spot" after each meal or drink of water.

2. When he relieves himself at the designated area, praise him enthusiastically.

3. Arrange for a relief stop after all long playtimes.

4. Schedule Hugo's last relief break as late at night as you possibly can.

5. The very first thing each morning, as early as possible, rush your puppy outside.

6. Plan on several relief breaks whenever you and Hugo are home together.

7. Be aware of the warning signs that a Pom puppy, or even an adult Pomeranian, displays when he needs to go outside:

✔ Hugo will have an anxious look on his face.

✔ He will begin circling in one spot, sniffing for the right place to relieve himself.

✔ In an obvious attempt to get your attention, Hugo will whine, whimper, and run toward the door.

✔ Your dog or puppy will begin to squat.

In Case of Accidents

✔ If Hugo can't hold back any longer, pick him up and go calmly (and quickly) to the outside relief spot. *Do this even if your dog has already had an accident.*

✔ Again, wait patiently (and quietly) at the relief spot until Hugo has relieved himself, then heap on the praise, thereby reinforcing the fact that he relieved himself at the right spot.

✔ Back inside, thoroughly clean the accident site and apply scent neutralizers (Nature's Miracle is one popular brand) that work on enzymes by actually eliminating the smell rather than masking or covering it up. Do this to each mistake spot to keep from sending false scent-signals about the right place for Hugo to urinate or defecate.

✔ Do not ever speak harshly or discipline Hugo at the relief spot. This spot should be the place where he knows exactly what to expect each time; he will relieve himself and get praised for doing so.

✔ As you go with Hugo to the relief spot, and as you wait for action at the site, be quiet! Play is for another time.

✔ *Never rub* your puppy's nose in any urine or stool! This is an old and stupid

myth that only results in a confused and soiled puppy.

✔ *Never strike* a puppy when he makes a mistake.

✔ Don't scream at a puppy that is not house-trained. You can make some noise, such as clapping your hands, to break an inappropriately defecating or urinating puppy's mindset or train of thought. Then hustle Hugo outside to the relief spot.

Consistency

Be consistent in all your house-training efforts. Make certain that all other household members are doing the same things that you are doing and in the same manner.

Note: Never just push a Pomeranian out the door, even into a safe, fenced backyard, to defecate or urinate alone. Your praise is the reward he gets for going in the specific spot each time he goes outside.

Paper Training

If you have to use a paper-training area inside your home, place your puppy's food and water as far away from the relief paper area as possible. Because paper training is less effective, continue to take your Pomeranian outside after meals and drinks and early in the morning and late at night.

Crate Training Hints

✔ Maintain a realistic and positive attitude about the use of crates or carriers and the positive role they can play in providing a "den" for your Pomeranian.

✔ Obtain a large enough crate or carrier to comfortably serve as a den for your Pom when he is an adult. (This is usually the smallest crate made!) Make a movable, temporary partition to keep the den just the right size as Hugo grows.

✔ Locate this den in an out-of-the-way, but not isolated, place in a part of the household that is always in use but away from any temperature fluctuations that would make it uncomfortable at times.

✔ Put Hugo in the crate for naps and when he must be left unattended for several hours. Upon your return, immediately take the puppy outside to the relief spot. Praise him when he defecates or urinates and go right back inside with him.

✔ Use the stern alpha-leader, authoritative voice to quiet any whining or barking that Hugo makes as he is being placed in the makeshift den.

✔ Do not praise him for about ten minutes after he is let out of the crate. Immediate praise will make getting out more of a reward to Hugo than you want it to be.

✔ During training, put him back in his den after he has spent about 30 minutes outside of it, and make him quiet down. Through consistent reinforcement, the amount of time you can leave Hugo in the den can be extended.

✔ Don't leave any dog, especially a younger animal, in a crate for an overly long period of time. Hugo won't be able to hold back his need to relieve himself and you will have a real mess to clean up.

✔ Always keep a mat or towel in the den along with a favorite chew toy to make it a comfortable place.

✔ In order to cut down on possible spillage, do not put food or water in the crate or carrier.

✔ Make sure your family and frequent visitors to your house fully understand the true purpose and actual importance of crate training and how it must be done.

INFORMATION

Clubs and Organizations

American Pomeranian Club*
National Breeder Referral
Jane Lehtinen
(218) 741-2117
Brenda Turner
Secretary
3910 Concord Place
Texarkana, TX 75501-2212
www.americanpomeranianclub.org

American Kennel Club (AKC)
5580 Centerview Drive
Raleigh, NC 27606-3390
www.akc.org

Canadian Kennel Club (CKC)
89 Skyway Avenue, Suite 100
Etobicoke, Ontario M9W 6R4
Canada
(416) 675-5511
www.ckc.ca

United Kennel Club (UKC)
100 E. Kilgore Road
Kalamazoo, MI 49001-5598
(616) 343-9020
www.ukcdogs.com

The Kennel Club
1-5 Clarges Street, Picadilly
London W7Y 8AB England
www.the-kennel-club.org.uk

American Boarding Kennel Association
4575 Galley Road, Suite 400-A
Colorado Springs, CO 80915
www.americanboardingkennel.com

*This address may change as a new officer
is elected. The latest listing can always be
obtained from the American Kennel Club.

Magazines

The American Kennel Club Gazette
American Kennel Club
51 Madison Avenue
New York, NY 10010
www.akc.org

Dog Fancy
P.O Box 53264
Boulder, CO 80323-3264
www.dogfancy.com

Dog World
29 North Wacker Drive
Chicago, IL 60606
www.dogworldmag.com

The Pom Reader
8848 Beverly Hills
Lakeland, FL 33809-1604

The Pomeranian Review
(The official publication of the American
Pomeranian Club)
102 Tudor Lane
Lansing, MI 48906

Books

Cunliffe, Juliette. *Pomeranian* (Comprehensive Owner's Guide). Allenhurst, NJ: Kennel Club Books, LLC., 2004.

Hughes, Pauline B. *The Pomeranian*. Springfield, MO: Denlinger's Publishers, 1990.

Rugh, Karla. *Barron's Dog Bibles: Pomeranians*. Book with DVD. Hauppauge, NY: Barron's Educational Series, Inc., 2010.

Tietjen, Sari Brewster. *The New Pomeranian*. New York: Howell Book House, 1987.

Vanderlip, Sharon, DVM. *The Pomeranian Handbook*. Hauppauge, NY: Barron's Educational Series, Inc., 2007.

About the Author

Joe Stahlkuppe is a widely read pet columnist, author, pet radio personality, and freelance feature writer. A long-time fan of purebred dogs, Joe Stahlkuppe has written 24 books and many hundreds of newspaper and magazine articles. He has written over a dozen of Barron's Pet Owner's Manuals. He lives near Birmingham, Alabama, with his wife, Cathie. He divides his time between his grandchildren, Ann Catherine, Peter, Julia, and Alexandra and his volunteer activities with the Jefferson County (AL) Board of Education, the Disabled Veterans of America, and the Vietnam Veterans of America.

Photo Credits

Norvia Behling: pages 35, 47, 48, 54, 56, 62, 66, 69, 82; Seth Casteel: pages 2–3, 4, 5, 7, 8, 10, 15, 21, 22, 24, 27, 28, 33, 37, 38, 51, 55, 59, 64, 78, 81, 87, 89; Kent Dannen: pages 6, 11, 19, 34, 45, 57, 58, 61, 68, 71, 74, 79, 80, 88, 92; Tara Darling: pages 13, 18 (top, bottom), 84; Cheryl Ertelt: page 20; Shirley Fernandez: pages 40, 60, 77; Isabelle Francais: pages 9, 32, 36, 42, 46, 50, 90; Daniel Johnson: pages 31, 52, 83, 85; Paulette Johnson: pages 30, 44; Pets by Paulette: page 49; Shutterstock: page 93; Kira Stackhouse: page 75.

Cover Photos

Shutterstock: front cover, back cover, inside front cover, inside back cover.

Important Note

This book is concerned with selecting and owning Pomeranians. The publisher and the author think it is important to point out that the advice and information for Pomeranian maintenance applies to healthy, normally developed animals. Anyone who acquires an adult dog or one from an animal shelter must consider that the animal may have behavioral problems and may, for example, bite without any visible provocation. Anxiety-biters are dangerous for the owner as well as the general public.

Caution is further advised in the association of children with dogs, in meeting with other dogs, and in exercising the dog without a leash.

Acknowledgments

I would like to thank Pat Hunter and Marcy Rosenbaum of Barron's for their excellent editorial work on *Pomeranians*. Thanks should also go to the countless reputable breeders of Pomeranians who have had to endure the difficulties and tragedies wrought by puppy mills and "teacup" Pom breeders.

This book is dedicated to the best young dog man that I have ever met, Darrin Mayfield, to Dr. Anna Vacca, and to all the other students and staff of Gardendale High School, Gardendale, Alabama.

© Copyright 2010, 2000, 1991 by Barron's Educational Series, Inc.

All rights reserved.
No part of this publication may be reproduced or distributed in any form or by any means without the written permission of the copyright owner.

All inquiries should be addressed to:
Barron's Educational Series, Inc.
250 Wireless Boulevard
Hauppauge, NY 11788
www.barronseduc.com

Library of Congress Catalog Card No. 2010014074

ISBN-13: 978-0-7641-4337-0
ISBN-10: 0-7641-4337-9

Library of Congress Cataloging-in-Publication Data
Stahlkuppe, Joe.
  Pomeranians / Joe Stahlkuppe.
    p. cm. — (A complete pet owner's manual)
  Includes bibliographical references and index.
  ISBN-13: 978-0-7641-4337-3 (alk. paper)
  ISBN-10: 0-7641-4337-9 (alk. paper)
  1. Pomeranian dog. I. Title.
  SF429.P8S73 2010
  636.76—dc22   2010014074

Printed in China

9 8 7 6 5 4 3 2 1